Get to Reach the Right People with LinkedIn

Generate contacts, get clients, search for jobs, and find distributors, partners, and investors.

First Edition 2017

Published by David Martínez Calduch

All rights reserved: David Martínez Calduch

ISBN-13: 978-1977560117

ISBN-10: 1977560113

SUCCESS IS NOT AN ACCIDENT.

It is hard work, perseverance, learning, study, sacrifice and, above everything else, love for what you do.

- Pelé

Acknowledgements

This book is the accumulation of knowledge gathered through study and practice in countless hours, to get to find out what are the right and most effective actions, in every work and project conducted for my company and for the clients, to whom I'm grateful for their confidence in me, and all the knowledge they have provided to me.

David Martínez Calduch

About the author

David Martínez Calduch

Social Selling and Digital Strategy Consultant.

Founder of 3 companies, trainer and international lecturer.

More than 25 years' experience in Information and Communication Technologies.

Executive MBA ESIC Business and Marketing School

Digital Transformation of the organizations.

Writer of several books:

http://amazon.com/author/davidmcalduch

28 years as in company trainer, Business Schools and Universities, in Spain and LATAM. Hootsuite Solution Partner, Hootsuite Ambassador, ECC Evernote Certified Consultant.

- **Twitter:**   https://twitter.com/davidmcalduch
- **Instagram:** https://instagram.com/davidmcalduch
- **Websites:**   https://www.solucionafacil.es

    https://www.davidmcalduch.com

LinkedIn Profile https://www.linkedin.com/in/davidmcalduch

Prologue

LinkedIn's huge potential, which I've been discovering through all these years of usage for my company and clients, has made me take the step of creating this book series called "The Keys of LinkedIn" to help the people who want to get the most out of it; for them to have a useful guide to be able to do it.

http://www.lasclavesde.com/linkedin

Within this series, you are now on the second book

- **Create an Efficient Profile to Achieve your Objectives with LinkedIn**

  o In the first book, you'll see all of the profile planning and creation, which is the corner stone of every work strategy on LinkedIn.

- **Get to Reach the Right People with LinkedIn**

  o In this book, I cover the contact network management, ways to contact, strategies, advanced searches, how to bypass limitations, Sales Navigator, and work with groups.

The work you do with this 2nd book is entirely based on all the work you've done with the 1st book, which is creating your profile (there're over 200 pages), so I recommend you start there.

When I say this is the second book, I mean that you can apply what you learn here independently and you will achieve something, but you'll lose effectiveness for not having done it right from the beginning.

Are you interested in achieving better results with the same amount of effort? Then follow the order of the books ;-)

This book follows the same idea as its predecessor; it's a practical book to keep next to the computer and apply everything, because only by applying it you will learn it, and get results.

Those contents I've explained in book 1, I won't repeat them here unless it's absolutely necessary to be able to do something I'm showing, since the area covered and the contents are completely different.

For you to easily access the web addresses that will appear in the book, and so it's easier for you to type them, I'll include a QR code in each one of them, for you to scan. Below, I'm putting two free apps, one for Android and the other for iOS, for you to scan the QR codes.

Android	iOS
Play Store QR Code Reader	Quick Scan - QR Code Reader
http://ow.ly/Yu2f30eyjCQ	http://ow.ly/J1Mb30eyjFx

Índice

Chapter 1

What We Can Get to Achieve

There are no limits, only obstacles,

and any obstacle can be overcome.

- David Belle

Actor, sportsman, and founder of the parkour foundation.

The only limit that exists when taking actions to reach the people you want to reach, is actually only marked by you. You are the limit; where you think you can get to, how far you believe in yourself to achieve, and how much you are willing to work to make it possible.

After all these years using LinkedIn both for my company and helping my clients achieve their objectives, my conclusion is that there is no limit to what can be achieved.

1.1 What is LinkedIn

LinkedIn is a professional network, focused on professional relations. Since LinkedIn's appearance, it has had remarkably high growth rates.

- 2003 May – LinkedIn is founded

- 2007 Sept - 14,000,000 members

- 2009 Oct - 50,000,000 members

- 2010 Feb - 60,000,000 members

- 2010 Jun - 70,000,000 members

- and 1,000,000 company profiles

- 2010 Nov - 85,000,000 members

- 2011 Feb - 100,000,000 members

- 2013   > 300,000,000 members

- 2017   500,000,000 members

There are two important milestones to highlight; in 2017, LinkedIn reached 500 million professionals signed up.

https://blog.linkedin.com/2017/april/24/the-power-of-linkedins-500-million-community

And on June 13 2016 Microsoft made the purchase of LinkedIn for 26,200 million de dollars, and it's being integrated with Office 365 and Microsoft Dynamics CRM.

https://blog.linkedin.com/2016/06/13/microsoft-and-linkedin

1.2 What Can I Achieve with LinkedIn

Besides what most people know (that LinkedIn is useful to find a job), LinkedIn has other benefits:

- Professional Career

  - Being in contact with coworkers and colleagues

  - Getting a job

  - Increasing your professional reputation / personal brand, improving your image within the company

  - Getting clients

- Company

  - Giving your company visibility

  - Giving your message a wider broadcast

  - Attracting talent

  - Export / Internationalize

- Locating Distributors / Partners

- Increasing sales

o Startup

- Making your project known

- Getting investors

- Hiring experts

The big question is: what do *you* want to achieve?

To be able to achieve our objectives, we must understand how LinkedIn works and which have to be the steps to follow in order to achieve them.

Let's imagine we're building a house. The first thing we need to do are the foundations, and that would be our LinkedIn Profile. And it's not about copying and pasting your resume or simply filling it up. You need to do a very good profile focused in your objectives. In this "LinkedIn on a Professional Level" series https://thekeysof.com/linkedin/ the first thing you should do is creating that super profile. I've made a book for that end, "Create an Efficient Profile to Achieve your Objectives with LinkedIn" https://amzn.to/2KaRMBW where I only explain how to create the profile, and it's over 200 pages long. It's really a lot more work than you may believe, and doing it right will make the actions you take later, which we'll see in this book, significantly increase the results ratio.

Once we've created a well done LinkedIn profile is when we must create a contacts agenda based on our objectives and the way of working we consider is best for us.

From there, we can start our work of searching, locating, and contacting the people in which we're interested, and doing a contents dissemination work.

You must stay with one idea: all the work you do is based on your agenda's potential, and it always gets to your profile, which the final key piece of everything.

I understand you've already done the profile work and now we're going to start the work.

Everything I show you from the computer will be shown with the English menus, since that's how you'll see every button (the rest of the language don't have them all), regardless of the language in which you have your profile.

If you're using a Tablet, I recommend you install Chrome and after entering www.linkedin.com select the Chrome menu and indicate you want to see it like the desktop version.

In the Smartphone App, you can use either iOS or Android, I recommend you look for updates so we always work with the latest version.

1.3 The Six Levels Theory

In a story called Chains, from 1930, written by Firdyes Karintyn, raised the theory of the six degrees of separation[1].

It raises a theory indicating that all the people in the world are connected by 6 levels. This means that, if you know one person (level 1), this person knows another (level 2), that person knows another (level 3), and so on, on 6 levels of people we'd be all connected.

---

[1] https://en.wikipedia.org/wiki/Six_degrees_of_separation

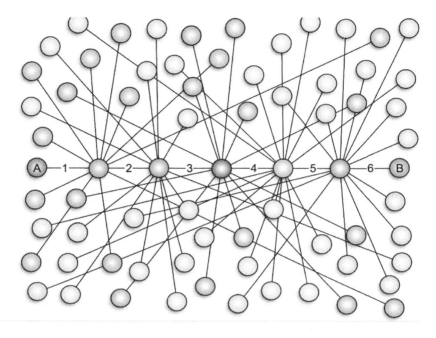

In the physical world, these 6 levels are impossible to discover. We'd have to gather every one of our acquaintances, ask them to give us a list of people they know, and arrange for them to do the same until you reach level 6. Madness; they'll believe we're out of our minds.

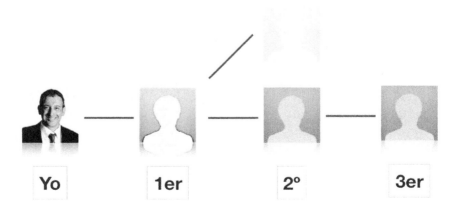

But on the digital world, everything changes, because there we can make part of that contacts network visible, and that's where LinkedIn can help us.

Those people we know in LinkedIn will invite us (or we'll invite them) and they'll be our Level 1. They're contacts (acquaintances) will be our Level 2. The contacts of our Level 2 people will be our Level 3 and are called Out of the Network. This is the way of structuring them and naming them in LinkedIn.

With the use of LinkedIn, you'll see that it even seems that we're connected to almost anyone in 4 levels.

Your clients and your next job are on Level 3.

- LinkedIn

1.4 The Potential of our Contacts Network

When we see the part of how to make searches, you'll see that the limitation is given by your contacts agenda for the reason below.

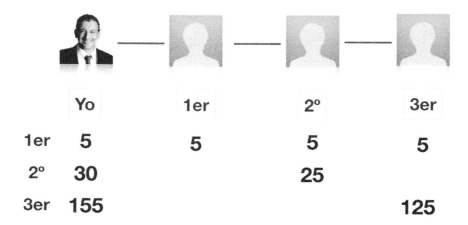

	Yo	1er	2°	3er
1er	5	5	5	5
2°	30		25	
3er	155			125

When we see the par on how to make searches, you'll see the limitation is given by your contacts network for this reason. If we have five Level 1 contacts, they have five contacts (Level 2) and they subsequently have five contacts (Level 3), when we do LinkedIn searches to locate people that interest you we can reach 155 people with 5 Level 1 contacts (the sum of Level 1 + Level 2 + Level 3).

In my case, I have over 10,000 Level 1 contacts, over 4 million people on Level 2, and you may imagine Level 3.

Don't stick to the idea of having to have a super agenda, or going trigger happy with the invites, it's not about that. Later on, you'll see strategies on how to do it in concordance with your objectives. I'm explaining this to you so you see the potential of the agenda when making searches.

1.5 Online and Offline Work Technique

Thanks to the digital world, all the social media and tools, messaging and videoconference apps, etc. we can do a lot of work without "moving". The world has now actually become a digital village.

But let's be honest, there are times when you meet with a person for 10 minutes face to face, you can figure them out, you're able to look at their eyes and see if there's feeling, or how they tick.

So, as digital as we can be, that Offline / Physical part is important. I'd say, the more technology we have, the more important the human relationships part is.

Físico

Virtual

As you can see in the illustration, this is the work I do, the people I know in real life, I invite them to LinkedIn, and the people I have as contacts in LinkedIn whom I'm interested to meet in person to comment on projects, I try to schedule a meeting with them in order to "de-virtualize" them.

1.5.1 From Physic to Virtual

The first part, adding the "Physical" people to the digital world of LinkedIn professional network, has two objectives I want to achieve.

1.5.2 Unblocking the Agenda

When we connect with other people on LinkedIn, these people have access to our agenda (if we don't block it), and we have access to their agendas (if they haven't blocked it).

Also, their Level 2 and 3 contacts network is added to our network when making searches, thus increasing our potential of reaching people. This increases the possibilities of being able to send a message to the people of a company in which we're interested.

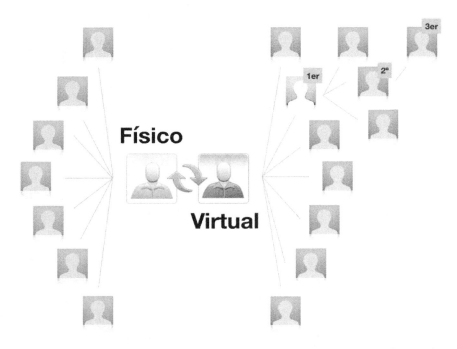

As you can see in the image, by passing a user from the physical world (blue) to our Virtual / Digital world (yellow), their Levels 1 and 2 become our Levels 2 and 3, participating in searches.

Later, you're going to learn the different strategies that exist for managing and creating our agenda, and how to combine between them.

1.5.3 Amplifying my Message's Signal

When we publish our own contents or external contents, these posts appear on their LinkedIn walls (Home), and we have the probability that our Level 1 contacts will see them.

If, besides, any of our Level 1 contacts interacts with the post (clicking Like, commenting, or sharing), our post is shown to their Level 1 contacts, which are our Level 2 contacts, widely increasing our reach.

Here we have an example of a post where most people that have seen it are our direct Level 1 contacts.

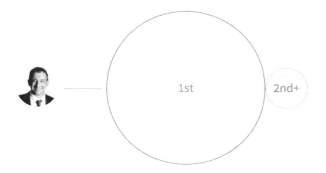

And now we have an example of a post where we've been able to overcome the Level 1 barrier so our content is seen by our Level 2.

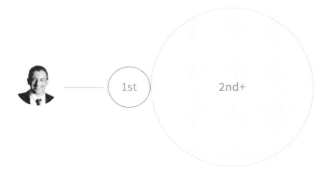

1.6 What Can We Do with each Level

Depending on the person being a Level 1, 2, 3, or out of network, we can do different things. The closer they are to us, the more we can do; send them messages, having our posts on their walls, looking through their agendas, etc. and the further we are, we may even not be able to see their photo, last names, or their profiles.

Here's a chart with each of the Levels and what we can do with each of them.

Level	Name	What we can do
1	First level contacts	Direct access, messages, seeing their agenda, phone and email.
2	Second level contacts	Access for invites
3	Third level	Where your next job and clients are, very complicated invitation.
>3	Out of network	Accessible with paid versions with InMail.

1.7 The Agenda Limit and How to Skip it

LinkedIn has established a limit for Level 1 of 30,000 contacts. From that moment, to be able to add a new Level 1 person, we need to delete another Level 1 person first.

The way to make more people to follow our posts (which is what our Level 1 contacts see) is a button that LinkedIn can add for us, which is "Follow".

If, for example, we're going to look at Mr. X's profile, it's going to be very hard to get him as a contact, because he doesn't know us and we don't have his email to invite him. So, we can Follow him to see all his posts on our LinkedIn home screen.

Chapter 2

Planning our Strategy

"The most important ingredient for success is knowing how to interact with people"

- Theodore Roosevelt
26th President of the United States

Now, what we're going to do is starting to work with LinkedIn. If you've already signed up, read this to see what you can improve, since I'm going to show you the methodology, I use here step by step.

If you haven't signed up yet, follow the guide I show you here to do it right from the beginning.

Now we're going to sign up to LinkedIn and we're going to do an overview of the sections before we dive in the profile creation.

First, you need to do a previous work to set the foundations of the work you're going to develop later.

2.1 Three Strategies for Contacts Management

There's a saying that goes «rush is a bad counselor», and as you may imagine, it's not about indiscriminately sending requests. Now I'm going to explain three strategies for the contacts agenda creation, you must choose the one that fits you most comfortably or make a combination of several.

It's not about which one is good or bad, or which is better or worse, it's about which one adapts better to you.

2.1.1 Strict

I only accept/invite people I know. It's the most restrictive one of all, since we don't accept anyone we don't know.

I have clients who manage their agenda like this, they're usually professionals with very high positions within large organizations and politicians.

This use is given for not using LinkedIn intensively, having a very important work load volume, and having LinkedIn mostly as a site where they can a have a professional digital presence.

The inconvenience I see with this approach is that, to be in touch with the people I already know, I don't need LinkedIn. For that I already have email, Slack, Telegram, WhatsApp, and others.

But, as I'm saying, everyone has to see which one adapts better to their objectives

2.1.2 Medium

I only accept/invite people I'm interested in. Here, we're in a position where we analyze each person who sends us an invite, and we decide if we're interested in them professionally. If that's the case, we accept it; if not, we click on ignore.

For most professionals, this would be the best strategy, since we sift the people we invite and accept. The intensity level in that contact sifting when accepting them will be entirely up to you.

Keep in mind that, if you're too strict, it'll narrow your search reach.

2.1.3 Open

I initially accept/invite everyone. This is the most open and indiscriminate option when accepting people; it would basically mean accepting everyone and going trigger happy with invites.

I don't believe this is the best option either, not by a long chalk.

2.1.4 The One I Use

In my case, I use a combination of several. On one side, when sending invites, if that person is in my agenda or database, I initially invite them all. Still, before sending the invites, I do a quick check in case there's punctually any person or persons I don't want to invite and I unmark them.

When inviting people based on searches, I'm very selective, because I'm looking for people for something concretely, and thus I'm selective and analyze their profiles before.

When I receive invitations, I'm very open to accept everyone since I give lectures and conferences, which gets me a lot of requests. But if I see something strange in their profile, I check it out and, if I spot something I don't like, I reject the invite.

2.2 Quantity vs Quality

Is it better to have a 25 contacts agenda or a 2000 one?

Well, like everything in life, it depends.

2000 contacts who have nothing to do with you, your professional career, nor your objectives, you may probably figure it's not a good strategy. And having 25 contacts, 100% focused on your objectives, is way better.

I must also tell you that, as a bare minimum, I recommend to at least have 150-200 contacts. The objective you should mark is getting to have at least 501 contacts, because then you may show you have over 500 contacts, without having to indicate the exact quantity you have, 501, 1,000 or 10,000.

David Martinez Calduch
Social Selling • Digital Marketing Strategist
Soluciona Facil • ESIC: Business & Marketing School
Valencia Area, Spain • 500+ ⧸⧸

2.3 Networkers or Super Connectors

Let's imagine that, when inviting people, we look for "Networkers" or "Super connectors", which are people who have a large contacts agenda.

With my current 10,000 contacts agenda, I'm allowed to reach 4,200,000 people on level 2.

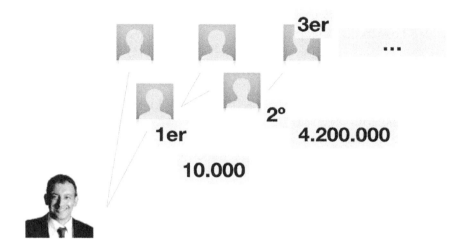

Let's imagine we connect with 3 people, with 10,000 contacts each, those are 30,000 new Level 2 contacts which will cause an exponential growth on our Level 3.

The objective you'd have to mark is for those Networkers' agendas to be aligned with you.

There are people who add the word LION or L.I.O.N. to their professional title or to their name, which means LinkedIn Open Network. Those are people who indicate they're open to accept invites and tend to have a lot of contacts. The question is if they filter those request or indiscriminately accept them all. The suitability of adding them or not would come from that.

There're also people who indicate the contacts quantity they have on their professional title or next to their name, for example 10000, 20000, or in the following way on a more American format, the K stands for thousands, making it 1K, 2K, 10K, 15K. When we cover searches, we'll see how to locate them.

2.4 Planning the Invites

Now we're going to see which people we can or should invite.

We're going to see the planning and on the next chapter you'll see how to do it, step by step.

2.4.1 First Action Group

We'll invite those people we already know. This will allow us to make our agenda grow in a quick way, doing it with people we've already been in contact with. They'll recognize us and in most cases they'll accept us as coworkers, former coworkers, bosses, classmates, professors, friends, and relatives.

From all of them, you'll choose who you want to invite and who you don't, it's up to you. We're going to see how to do this step by step on the next chapter.

2.4.2 Own Sources

The second phase of invites, we'll do it using our own email sources.

The way LinkedIn establishes you know someone is because you have their email, the one they used for signing up to LinkedIn (which may be the one they used for registering or other – see the book "**Create an Efficient Profile on LinkedIn to Achieve your Objectives: The Keys to Stand Out and Being Visible: Volume 1 (The Keys of LinkedIn)** Chapter 8 "Profile – Contact Information", Item 8.3 "emails"). http://amzn.to/2C0FhE0

So we'll connect your email contacts from the different email accounts you have: Gmail, G-Suite, Office 365, Outlook, etc. and your iOS and Android devices.

We can also import the emails we have from other sources, like CRMs, newsletters, billing, etc.

2.4.3 Based on our Interests

We'll start working on searches to reach the contacts we want to reach.

Remember the effectiveness of this will come from your profile's quality and how well you know how to connect.

Within these searches, we have advanced, automatic, and Sales Navigator powered.

Which people should we look for? :

- Potential clients

- Recruiters (if you're looking for a job or may be looking for one in the future)

- Very active profiles

- Contacts within our industry or sector

- Experts in your industry or sector

- Etc.

2.4.4 Seeding Mode

If we promote our profile views, we'll manage to make our agenda slowly grow.

How many emails do you send in a year?

Include your public profile address in your emails signature, and generate more visits in your profile and thus more invites.

It's free and it doesn't take any effort; you'll achieve diffusion without moving a finger.

Chapter 3

Widening our Contacts Agenda

The best way of making our contacts agenda grow, to begin with, is starting to connect with those people we already know, so we're going to go step by step so you can start generating your contacts agenda.

We're going to do the whole process from a computer, and then from a Smartphone.

3.1 Contacts Pre-Load, Computer

LinkedIn recommends loading up to 500 contacts. If it loads all your contacts without problems, perfect; if not, you'll have to do it in clusters. The three only details LinkedIn needs are "First Name", "Last Name" and "Email Address".

We enter www.linkedin.com and, on the top right menu section we have "My Network".

By clicking it, we'll enter a screen which features the following section on the left part of the screen.

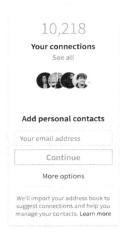

The last option is "More options", we click it so the following screen appears.

This URL will take you to that screen directly.

https://www.linkedin.com/mynetwork/import-contacts/

On the right section, you'll see how some email services appear so we can select them and add our email. We're going to cover them individually.

3.1.1 Gmail

The first one we'll do in case you have a Gmail account. Regardless of it being a particular or professional account, you don't need to worry, because LinkedIn won't invite anyone; you'll be the one who selects who to invite.

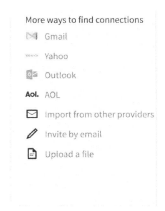

Now you have to click the first "Gmail" icon. When you do that, this screen will appear.

Now you must add your email account and your password. If you have already logged in your email accounts, a screen like this one may appear.

When you enter your account info, LinkedIn loads your contacts agenda, and looks for people who have signed up to LinkedIn with those emails. If it matches, it deems that you know them. You'll see how the page loads.

See who you already know on LinkedIn
The fastest way to grow your network is to import your contacts

Your email address

Continue

We'll import your address book to suggest connections. Learn more

Find more connections like Roberto, Sandra and César.

This load may take some time depending on the amount of emails you have, you have to be a little patient, because if you leave that screen, you'll have to start over.

Once it's done, a screen showing those people found in LinkedIn within your email contacts agenda, which would mean you know them, will appear.

Step 1 of 2

We're now on the step 1 of 2, which is indicated on the top right section of this screen.

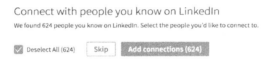

As you can see, it indicates there are 624 people we have on our emails agenda, which have signed up to LinkedIn and we can invite them to add them to our agenda if we want, making them our Level 1.

If you click the blue "Add connections" button, you'll invite them all in one click. I recommend you go through the list and unmark (don't invite) those people you don't want as your Level 1; competence, people you're not in good sync with, etc.

Next to each person, you have a checkbox to mark and unmark if you want to invite them or not. When you're done, now you can press the blue "Add connections" button.

On that very moment, LinkedIn will send an invite to every single person whose box you left marked, and invitation for them to add you to their contacts agenda. In a matter of hours you'll see people starting to accept you, and in a few days you'll see how your agenda has quickly grown with people you know.

This is due to all those people already having signed up to LinkedIn and most of them having the LinkedIn app installed on their Smartphones, and they get a notification of your request on their Smartphone, so the acceptance process is only checking who you are and clicking on accept.

Step 2 of 2

Now we're going to start the Step 2 of 2. In this step, it shows us all the emails we have in our contacts agenda, which LinkedIn didn't find signed up to LinkedIn.

You can see it indicates me I have 2,417 emails of people who aren't already on LinkedIn. I recommend you Skip step 2. The reason of that is, if you invite them, you'll have over 2,400 people who'll ask you what LinkedIn is, how to sign up, etc.

Step 1 of 2 is interesting, but I never do the step 2 of 2.

Now, repeat this process with every Gmail account you have. If it connects you directly to the Gmail account you just did and it doesn't ask for your email and password, open a new window on your browser, go to https://mail.google.com and logout from Gmail, so it asks for your email and password when you repeat the process.

3.1.2 G Suite / Google Apps

Gmail service for companies, now called G Suite and previously Google Apps, can also be connected.

You must follow the same steps you just followed on the previous item.

3.1.3 Yahoo and AOL

If you have any address with one of those two services, you must click on the icon and repeat the steps we've done, for each and every email account you have

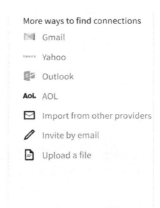

3.1.4 Outlook Windows Desktop 2007

If your Outlook version is a version installed on your own computer, what you have to do is exporting your contacts agenda to upload it to LinkedIn so it can do the whole process.

To do that, you must follow these steps.

Open Outlook in your computer and click on the "File" menu.

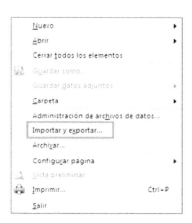

Select he "Import and export…" option

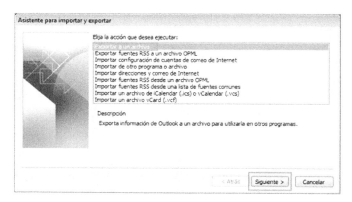

This screen will appear, we must select the first option "Export to a file" and click on "Next".

Now we select "Values separated by tabulations (Windows)" and we click on Next.

We've already indicated Outlook which kind of format we want to create; it's called CSV format, and now we have to select our contacts agenda so it can be exported and the file can be generated.

Browse the explorer Outlook will open, select "Contacts" and click on "Next". In that moment, it will ask you to name the file (don't use special characters, accents, and don't use a very long name), and save it to a folder where it's easy to locate (downloads, documents, etc.)

In that moment, the export process will begin. Remember, the time it takes will depend on the size of your contacts agenda.

When it's done, we'll have exported our contacts agenda with the data it had thus far in a file.

The next step we must take is uploading that file to LinkedIn so it can tell us who's on LinkedIn and who isn't, so we can decide who we want to invite

We go to www.linkedin.com and we click on "My Network".

We click on "More options".

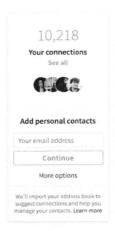

And now, in this screen, we select the "Upload a file" option on the right.

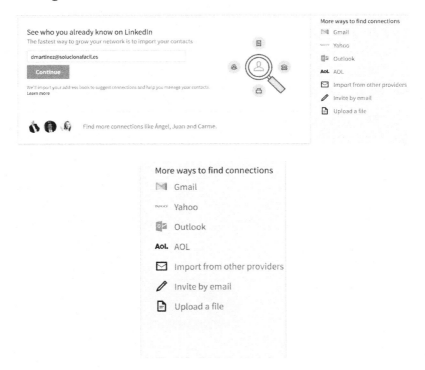

When we click it, a browsing window will appear so you can look for the CSV file in your computer. Look for it, select it, and click the "open" button, and the 2 Steps process we saw before will start.

3.1.5 Outlook Windows Desktop 2010

Open your Outlook and click on the "File" menu.

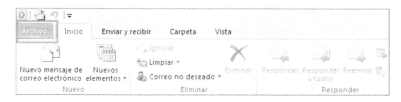

Select "Options".

This options screen will appear; select "Advanced".

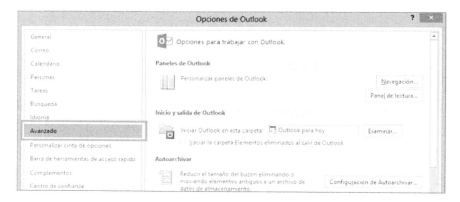

In the "Export" section, you must select the "Export" option.

Now the same assistant we've seen on Outlook's previous point will appear; select the file type, where the contacts agenda is, where to save the file, and load it to LinkedIn.

3.1.6 Outlook Windows Desktop 2013-2106

Open your Outlook and click on the "File" menu.

Now select "Open and Export" from the menu's left, and on the right you select "Import or Export".

And now you must follow the steps we've seen on point 3.1.1.4

3.1.7 Outlook Windows Desktop 365

To export your Office 365 contacts you must add your Office 365 email address to the Outlook desktop app.

Outlook Desktop will synchronize with the Office 365 inbox, and in some time you'll see you have a copy of your email and your contacts on the Outlook app.

Now you can follow the steps on point 3.1.1.6 to export your contacts agenda

3.1.8 Outlook Mac Desktop 2010

Open Outlook on your Mac and select the option "File", and select "Export". The assistant will appear; you select "Contacts". And now you can follow the steps on point 3.1.1.4.

3.1.9 Outlook Mac Desktop 2016

Open Outlook on your Mac and select the "File" option.

If it doesn't have the "Export" button, you must upgrade to Outlook latest version for Mac. If you see it, click on "Export".

The following screen will appear. Select "Contacts", and indicate the name of the file and where you want to save it.

And now you can do the file loading process we've seen on point 3.1.1.4.

3.1.10 Mac Agenda

First, I'm going to explain the formats Max uses for contacts. In order to export one or more contacts, they use the standard vCard format, and they also have the .abbu format option, which is a complete copy of the whole contacts agenda.

As you can see, neither of those options is the CSV format we need to upload the contacts to LinkedIn. LinkedIn admits three types of file formats for the upload: CSV, TXT, and VCF (vCard), which is the one we're going to use.

And this screen will appear.

We click on the first contact and we press the key combination Command + A to select all.

Then we go to the "File" menu / "Export" / "Export vCard".

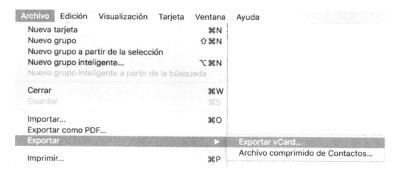

When we select the option, it'll show this screen where it asks for the file name and where we want to save it.

When you click the "Save" button it'll start creating the file; the time it takes will depend on the size of your agenda.

Now you must go to LinkedIn and upload the file so it can locate the people you know who have already signed up to LinkedIn.

3.1.11 Mac Mail

One of the best things about Mac OSX is that apps that are well developed for Mac use date in a centralized way, and this is done by Mail; the contacts agenda is the one incorporated in the Mac, so you have to do what I commented on point 3.1.10.

3.1.12 iCloud Mac

Open Safari on your Mac, go to www.icloud.com and enter your email and password to enter.

On the options menu that will appear, click on "contacts".

Now, a list with all of your contacts will show; we click on the first one, and it'll be highlighted in blue.

We press the key combination Command + A to select them all, and you'll see how they're all highlighted in blue.

Now, on the bottom left, we click on the gear icon and a menu will drop down, we select export vCard.

It will automatically download a file to our downloads folder, like this one.

vCards de iCloud
.vcf

The time it takes to create the file will depend on the size of your contacts agenda. Same as the previous point, you can now go to LinkedIn to upload the file.

3.1.13 Thunderbird

Open your Thunderbird email app:

1. Click on the Addresses Book.

2. Select the addresses book you wish to export.

3. Go to Tools and click on Export.

4. Click on "Format" and select ".CSV separated by commas".

5. Select the file name you want and where you want to save it.

6. Go to LinkedIn and upload the file, and you can now do the process described on point 3.1.1.4.

3.1.14 Other Sources

If your email uses another online email provider, you can try the "Import from other providers" option.

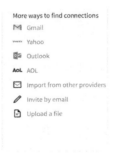

And this field will appear so you can enter your email, click "Continue" and it'll ask for your password.

If it worked, now you must follow the steps we saw on point 3.1.1.4, and if it didn't work, you must export the agenda to a CSV, TXT or VCARD format and upload the file.

3.1.15 Manual Invites

A very interesting option LinkedIn offers us is the possibility of sending invites to people through their emails, simply copying and pasting the addresses.

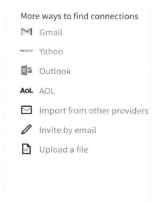

The second to last option is "Invite by email", we click it and this screen will appear, from the bottom right corner, we can click and drag to make the field bigger.

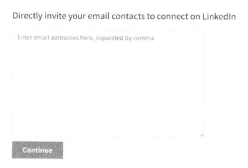

The way to introduce the emails is separating them with commas:

mail1@server.com, mail 2@server.com, mail 3@server.com, mail 4@server.com

You can type or copy + paste emails, one by one or several at a time.

We're going to see a way to use this option, which I tell you, I see it really interesting.

 The objective is adding a person or several people we've met as a Level 1 contact LinkedIn, so they'll see our LinkedIn profile, and can get to see our posts on LinkedIn.

 Let's imagine we email with someone back and forth, and it's in our interest to connect via LinkedIn (a possible client, a supplier, a partner, etc.), the only thing we need to do is copying their email, coming to this screen, paste it, and clicking on "Continue"; easy as that.

Let's supposed you get summoned to a meeting, and in the call you have the emails of all the people who will participate; you copy all the emails, paste them, and click "Continue".

As you can see, inviting people you have a professional relation with, is very easy, and you'll create your contact agenda step by step.

3.2 Smartphone Contacts Pre-Load

Another place where we have many contacts with their emails, is our smartphone. We're going to see how to tell LinkedIn to browse the people we have in our Smartphone (with email) so they can tell us if they've signed up to LinkedIn, and then you can decide whom you want to invited and whom you don't.

LinkedIn App for iOS	LinkedIn App for Android
https://itunes.apple.com/es/app/linkedin/id288429040?mt=8	https://play.google.com/store/apps/details?id=com.linkedin.android&hl=es

Install the App on your Smartphone, enter your LinkedIn email and password, and we're ready to start.

In the App menu, the second icon (the icon with two people), we click it, and "Add Contacts" will appear on the top right section; we click that.

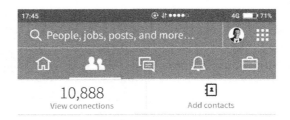

Now LinkedIn will browse through the emails to see who we know.

Now we're going to do the step 1 of 2, where it shows us those people we know because we have their email.

If you click the "Connect to All" button, it'll send an invite to everyone on the list.

I recommend you check the list, and click the "Connect" button next to every contact you wish to invite; once you're done, above everything on the right you'll see the "Skip" button to go to the next screen.

Now we're on step 2 of 2, which are the emails you have of people who aren't signed up on LinkedIn.

You can see how it indicates I have 1805 emails of people who haven't signed up, or who have signed up with another email.

On this screen, at the most, look for someone you're punctually interested in inviting, and then press the "Done" button on the upper right.

3.3 Troubleshooting

3.3.1 I don't know which Outlook version I have

If you don't know which Outlook version you have, you must go to the "File" menu and then click on "About…", where it'll indicate you which Outlook version you have installed.

3.3.2 I can't export my Outlook Agenda

Depending on the security policies installed on your company's computers, it's possible you don't have the necessary permissions to perform the exportation. Contact your IT Department so they can perform the exportation for you.

3.3.3 LinkedIn doesn't load my agenda

If your contacts agenda is too big, it's possible that LinkedIn can't load, or the loading step may take forever.

To solve it, what you need to do is divide the CSV in pieces, export the contacts agenda again, but this time select the contacts starting with the letter A-B-C, make another file for D-E-F, and so on until you export the whole agenda.

Now you must upload each one of the files individually.

3.3.4 Mac vCard upload doesn't work

If you see that you can't upload the vCard file you've generated, maybe it's because it's too big. Try creating it selecting only a part of the agenda. If it still causes trouble, try converting the vCard file to CSV.

Now, what we're going to do is converting this .vCard file into CSV. To do that, we go to this URL; the maximum file size admitted is 8 MB.

http://labs.brotherli.ch/vcfconvert/

Click "Select file", a window will open so you can select the file we just created.

In "Format", we select we want it to export the file in CSV.

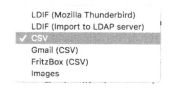

We select the rest of the options as I show you next.

vCard-File:	Seleccionar archivo Contacto y otras 3.770.vcf	(max. 8 MB)
Format:	CSV ◊ Tab ◊ ☑ Add header line	
Encoding:	Unicode (UTF-8) ◊	
Filter:	☑ vCards with e-mail only	
	☑ vCards with phone numbers only	
Modifications:	replace this International Access Code with «0»	

We click the "Convert" button and it'll generate a CSV file we can now upload to LinkedIn.

3.4 The Sword of Damocles

I don't want you to get the wrong idea about managing invites, nor give you the idea of going trigger happy with the invites, with the final goal of generating a large contacts agenda to be able to do better searches.

One of the objective usages LinkedIn pursues is avoiding Spam, which is one of the things LinkedIn users are most sensible about, and avoiding bad practices.

To face these issues, LinkedIn has an internal system with parameters to spot an abusive usage of the system. If you make X invites in 24 hours, etc. LinkedIn will indicate you that you can't invite nobody else until X hours have passed, etc.

Some of the limitations can be, for example, that it won't let you invite more people, because LinkedIn says you have many invites pending, you've invited too many people, and these haven't still accepted or rejected your invites, and you have two options: wait until the accept you so you can invite more people, or withdrawing some of the invites from long ago so you can use them on other people.

Another issue, even more serious, is that some people may have indicated they don't want you as a contact, but also told LinkedIn they don't know you. You'll see this in more depth on point 3.5.4

3.5 Invites

I don't want you to get the wrong idea of how to manage the invites part, nor give you the idea of going trigger happy with the invites, with the final goal of generating a large contacts agenda to be able to do better searches.

3.5.1 How to invite

3.5.1.1 From the Profile

To be able to invite someone, it's as easy as visiting their LinkedIn profile, and in the main "Connect".

When you click this button to Connect / Invite a person, both from the computer and a Smartphone, the text sent is one that LinkedIn always writes the same.

This won't work in every case, let's see an example, where I visit Guy Kawasaki's profile from a Smartphone.

As you can see, the "Connect" button isn't there. This happens for several reasons, either because the person is an Influencer (determined by LinkedIn), or because he's a Level 3 or out of the network. When one of this situations is given, when we visit that person's profile a button called "InMail" may appear, which we'll see later (paid invites), or "Following".

"Following" means we can follow this Influencer's posts and they can appear on our LinkedIn home, even if we're not Level 1 contacts.

If we still would like to invite this person, we can do so like this:

On a Smartphone, when we're looking at the person's profile, you'll see a button with three dots on the top right.

When we click it, this screen appears, where we have the "Connect" button. This option doesn't always work, since LinkedIn establishes limitations.

3.5.1.2 From Search

Another way of connecting with people is through searches, which we'll analyze in depth in a further chapter.

Let's see a search example with the query "Social Selling" from a Smartphone. The people who are already Level 1 contacts will appear with an icon to message them on the right, we'll see this in the next chapter. And if you take a look at "Perry van

Beek", they have the icon of a person with a plus sign that we can press to directly send them an invite.

By touching it and sending the invite, it'll look like this.

The same happens in the searches we perform from a computer. Instead of icons, the "Message" and "Connect" buttons will appear, and the work the same way as we saw on the Smartphone.

3.5.2 Customizing your Invite

As we commented, when we click on "Connect", both in the computer and Smartphone, LinkedIn writes a standard text saying we want to add that person to our contact network.

But there are times we would like to customize that invite message to create a customized message, indicating the reason why we wish to connect with them, etc.

3.5.2.1 Smartphone

To do it, when we're at the person's profile (you can't do so from the search), in the Smartphone screen, we press the upper right button with the three dots icon.

And this menu will show.

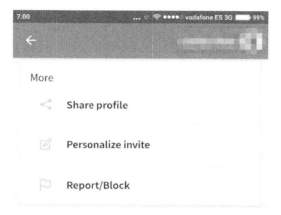

And we have the "Personalize invite" option; we click it, and the next screen will give us a maximum of 300 characters to personalize the text of the invite that the other person will receive.

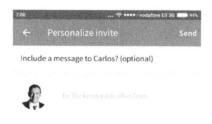

If we try this with an Influencer or a Level 3 contact, this screen will appear, where the first thing it asks is for you to indicate the address of the person you're inviting so you can prove you know them, and if you don't, you can't send the invite.

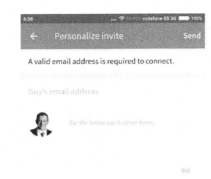

If we try to do this same action with this Influencer from a computer.

Surprise, there's no button to send a personalized invited.

3.5.2.2 Computer

When we click the "Connect" button from a computer, both in search...

… as if we did from within the LinkedIn profile.

When we click it, this screen will show, where indicates us if we want to send the invite directly with the automatic text, or if we want to customize it.

You can customize this invitation	✕

LinkedIn members are more likely to accept invitations that include a personal note.

Add a note   Send now

If we click the "Add a note" button, it'll show us this screen so we can type the customized text the other person will receive.

You can customize this invitation	✕

Include a personal message (optional):

Ex: We know each other from…

300

Cancel   Send invitation

3.5.3 Skipping Limitations

As we're seeing, LinkedIn establishes new limitations and there are ways of skipping them, which work momentarily, but in any given moment can stop working.

Depending on the steps we've taken to reach this contact, LinkedIn determines if they'll make things easy or hard for us to be able to invite them.

When we perform searches and the people list appears, you may sometimes find your invites limited. If you do it and it all goes right, perfect.

There are times when we visit a person's profile and, when we try to invite us, it gives us trouble (it limits us), and if we make a search for this person to appear, it's possible they let you invite them from the search list.

Another different way to access a profile which sometimes helps us invite them is going to Google and making a search like this one: "linkedin david Martinez Calduch".

https://www.google.es/?gfe_rd=cr&ei=iAxnWY-MEbKp8wefj6BA#q=linkedin+david+martinez+calduch

Indicating "linkedin" as the first word, the first thing that'll show up will be that person's LinkedIn profile. We click the link, and we've arrived to their profile directly and, even if sometimes it didn't allow us to visit it, now we can.

Now you see there are many ways we need to test and see the right way to get there.

At this moment, and I'll say how it is, at this moment, if you still have trouble to invite a person, visit that person from a Smartphone and, in most cases, you will be able to invite them.

3.5.4 Managing Invites. Computer

LinkedIn provides us with a screen where we can see all the invites we've received and are pending, and all the invites we've sent (accepted and pending).

3.5.4.1 Main screen

We go to www.linkedin.com and, on the top menu we click on "My Network".

And this zone will appear on the center of the screen where it shows the invites other people have sent to us; people who want to connect with us.

In this case, I don't want to accept the first person so, instead of clicking "Accept", I click "Ignore". In that moment, on the bottom left of the screen, LinkedIn shows us this message.

It informs us the invite has been rejected and eliminated, but below it also says "I don't know this person", which we can click so we can indicate we don't know this person. In this case, I won't click it.

If several people reject your invites and click that button to indicate they don't know you, you're going to be in serious trouble. LinkedIn is very concerned in preventing bad practices and Spam; they may take away your "Connect" button so you don't disturb more people, they can block your account, and even delete it.

This is one of the reasons why I say you can't go trigger happy with the invites, and we need to do things right.

3.5.4.2 Managing received invites

On the top right of this screen with the invites, we have the "Manage all" option.

Since I rejected the other invite, there's only one invite pending. On the top right, we still have the buttons "Ignore" and "Accept", and on the top left, we're on the "Received" tab and we also have the "Sent" tab, which we'll see in the next point.

3.5.4.3 Managing sent invites

If we click on the "Sent" tab, we'll see the list of all the invites we've sent. They're sorted by date, with the most recent ones on top, and the oldest at the bottom.

As you can see, the first one that shows up (most recent) is the invite we just sent to Perry. If we now wanted to withdraw the invite, we have the "Withdraw" button on the right.

If you're having trouble in LinkedIn because it sends you a warning that you have too many pending invites or can't send any more invites, you can come here, go all the way down (oldest invites) and withdraw a few.

3.5.5 Managing Invites. Smartphone

From the renovated LinkedIn App for Smartphones we can also manage the invites we get.

3.5.5.1 Main Screen

On the app's main screen, we click the contacts icon, the second icon from left (the icon with two people).

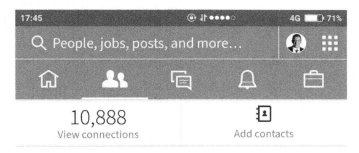

When we click it, this screen will appear where it shows us people we may know. On the top we see "No pending invites" and on the right we see "MANAGE ALL".

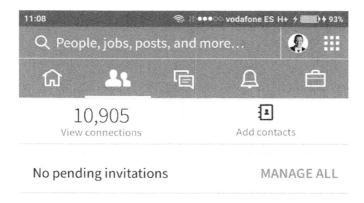

3.5.5.2 Managing received invites

If we click "MANAGE ALL" we can manage our received invites.

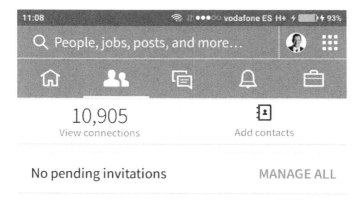

On the screen that appears, we click on the left, "RECEIVED, and the invites we've sent will appear.

No pending invitations

3.5.5.3 Managing sent invites

If we click "MANAGE ALL" we can manage our sent invites.

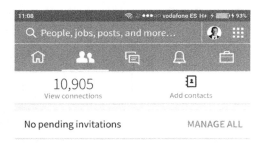

On the screen that appears, we click on the top "SENT", and it'll show us, just like in a computer, the list of invites we've sent. Nest to each one, on the right, we have the "WITHDRAW" button.

3.6 Writing a good invitation

If you want to increase the invite ratio, the key lies on customizing the invite depending on the person we're addressing.

When structuring how to focus the invite text, we must classify in which group the person whom we're going to send the invite is:

1. Coworkers.

2. Former coworkers.

3. Someone you've met.

4. Contact from Networking or an event.

5. A person from a LinkedIn group.

6. Classmates.

7. Recruiters.

8. Investors.

9. Someone you want to work with.

10. Someone you admire or look up to.

You need to give each one of them a different approach.

Examples (don't copy-paste them; adapt them to your way of communicating, make them your own):

1. "Hello ____, I'm____ from the____ department, I'm sending you this invite so we can connect through LinkedIn. Best regards."

2. Hello ____, I'm not sure if you remember me, we worked together on ____; I was in the ____ position. I'm inviting you so we can keep in touch.

3. Hello ____, we met the other day on ____, and I'd like to connect to keep in touch. Best regards."

4. Hello ____, it was nice to meet you at the ___ event. Our conversation about ____ was interesting. Let's connect so we can keep in touch."

5. Hello ____, I've noticed we're on the same LinkedIn group ___ and I saw your comments about ___. I'd like to connect so we can further speak about that topic."

6. Hello ____, I located you while browsing LinkedIn, I'm ___, we were classmates at ___, I'm sending you an invite so we connect and don't lose track. Regards."

7. Hello ____, I see you work in ___. I'm in the ___ industry, I've been in this sector __ years. I'm inviting you to connect, and if you have some time, we can discuss if you have any open opportunity for someone with my experience. Thank you."

8. Hello ____, I've noticed you're an investor, I'd like to connect with you because I have a ___ project and I would like to know your opinion. Thanks a lot for your help."

9. Hello ____, I've been browsing your profile and I'm very impressed with your career. Please, accept my invite so we can connect; I'd like to speak with you."

10. Hello Mr. /Mrs. ____, I admire your work, which I've been following for a long time. It'd be an honor for me that you accept my invite to keep

track of your posts and be in touch with you. Best regards."

Other generic examples you can use:

- Show interest on something the other person is interested in.

    o "I've read your blog and I really like the last entry you posted"

    o "I have your book and I've been meaning to comment" (only something positive, any doubt or question you may have)

    o "I wanted to congratulate you on ___" (an achievement, award, success, press appearance, new position, etc.)

    o "I've seen you company has achieved ___ and I wanted to congratulate you"

    o "I want to congratulation on your ___" (Degree, masters, PhD, certification, etc.)

    o "I haven't heard from you in a long time, how's your family?"

- Look for things in common

    o "I saw you profile while searching for classmates. I noticed we went to the same university"

    o "I noticed you know ___, he/she's a partner of mine"

Chapter 4

Managing your Contacts Agenda

*If you work just for money, you'll never make it,
but if you love what you're doing and you always
put the customer first, success will be yours.*

- Ray Kroc

O nce our invites have been accepted, these people will now be our Level 1 contacts and will be added to our contacts agenda.

In this chapter, we're going to learn how to manage this agenda; in the free version, the paid version, with Sales Navigator, and exporting this agenda to other apps outside LinkedIn.

Due to the great amount of changes LinkedIn is performing, I'll include some screenshots from the former version, where you'll be able to see many more options which, at least momentarily, are now gone.

4.1 Managing from a computer

On LinkedIn computer screen we click on contacts.

He amount of Level 1 contacts we have will appear on the left, now we click the "See all" button.

10,898

Your connections

See all

4.1.1 Screen general overview

Now we've reached the main screen where we can manage all of our Level 1 contacts.

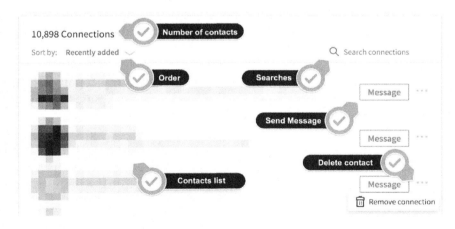

On the top right we have "Search connections", which is a browser where we type the word to search, and it only looks through our Level 1 contacts. We'll see a different way of doing it on the searches chapter.

4.1.2 Organizing the view

On the top we have the amount of contacts, right below we have a drop-down menu to determine how we want the contacts to be sorted.

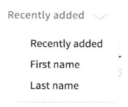

We have three options:

- • Recently added: the contacts that just became a Level 1 contact will appear on top. This way of sorting them is very interesting since we can see who the new contacts are so we can message them, see what we can offer, etc.

- • First name: alphabetically sorted list, it can be practical to locate a contact.

- • Last name: same as the last one, except it's sorted by last names.

4.1.3 Searching contacts

Q Search connections

On the top right we have "Search connections"; it's a browser where we type the word to search, and it only looks through your Level 1 contacts. We'll see a different way to do it on the searches chapter.

4.1.4 Sending messages

On the right of each contact is the "Message" button to message this person. We'll see this more in depth later.

4.1.5 Eliminating contacts

On the right of each contact there are two buttons: "Message" for sending messages, which'll see later, and three grey dots next to it. If we click on them, the "Remove connection" options appears.

If you click it, you remove that person from your contacts agenda, and that person will pass from being a Level 1 contact to a Level 2. The other person won't receive a notification.

Going from Level 1 to Level 2, they will no longer be able to message you, won't have access to your contacts agenda, and won't be able to see your email and phone number in your profile.

4.1.6 Labeling and organizing contacts

Before the interface revamp in 2017, LinkedIn allowed us to label our contacts in the free version to better manage them, and also to manage these labels.

In this moment, that option is not available in every Premium paid version. In order to have this labeling option, we must hire Sales navigator (Premium version for salespersons).

4.1.7 Exporting contacts

We have this option on the top of the contacts management screen.

📖   Manage synced and imported contacts

If we click it we'll get to a screen where we can export a file with all our contacts. This is the URL for that screen:

https://www.linkedin.com/mynetwork/contacts/

And on the bottom right we have this option:

Advanced actions

↑   Export contacts

↻   Manage contacts syncing

We click "Export contacts" and it'll take us here:

https://www.linkedin.com/psettings/member-data

Now we have two options, a quick download or the second, which is all of our LinkedIn data. It'll generate a file and they'll send it to us within 24 hours.

With the contacts file already exported, we can import it to our CRM, mailing platform, etc.

4.1.8 Managing sources and synchronization

Following the same steps as before from the contacts management screen, we click on:

📖 Manage synced and imported contacts

And we select "Manage contacts syncing".

Advanced actions

↥ Export contacts
↻ Manage contacts syncing

And we'll get to this screen:

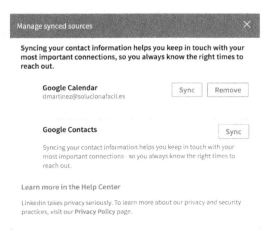

In this moment, LinkedIn allows us to automatically synchronize our LinkedIn account contacts and the calendar.

But, if we compare it to the previous version before all the changes LinkedIn is introducing, you can see many options have disappeared. We'll have to wait to see if they can be incorporated again.

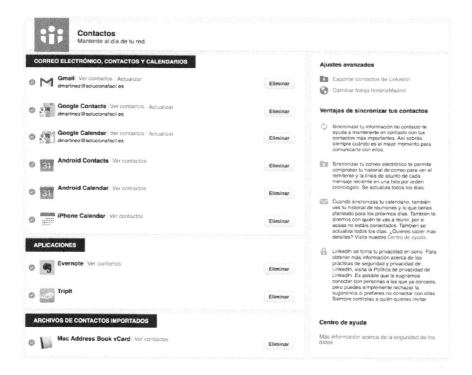

On the previous version we could connect Gmail / G Suite (email, contacts, and calendar), Android (contacts and calendar), iOS Calendar, Evernote contacts, Tripit and Mac contacts agenda.

4.2 Managing from a Smartphone

We open our LinkedIn app in our Smartphone and we're going to see how to manage contacts.

4.2.1 Screen overview

We've now arrived to the main screen where we can manage all our Level 1 contacts.

This is the app menu. If you have Android you'll see at the top, and if you have iOS you'll see it at the bottom, but they're the same buttons and functions.

The second button is where we come in (the icon with two people), which is for managing contacts. When we click it, this screen appears.

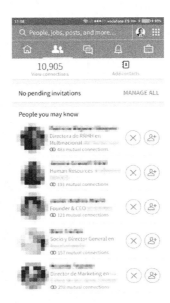

On the top it shows the amount of contacts we have, on the right we have "Add contacts", which we've already seen how it works, and below we have "MANAGE ALL" to manage the invites.

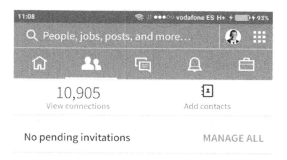

The section below are the contacts that LinkedIn recommends to us because it thinks they can interest us, for example, because we have connections in common. If you want to invite them, press the button with the person icon and the +, and if you don't want them to be recommended again (which isn't the same as deleting them), click the X. If you want to know more about that person, click on their name and you'll be able to see their profile (that person will know you've visited their profile).

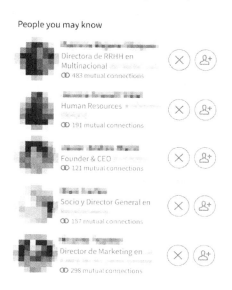

If we click on the amount (in my case 10,905) we'll go to the screen where we'll see all of our Level 1 contacts.

As you can see, it indicates the date where they became a Level 1 contact below each contact.

4.2.2 Sorting the view

On the top right we have a button that, if we click it

it'll show the same menu that appears on a computer to indicate how we want to see the contacts.

4.2.3 Searching contacts

Unlike in a computer, there isn't the option of searching only among our Level 1 contacts from the contacts screen; we have to do a global search from the option on the top of the Smartphone screen.

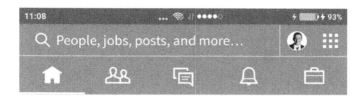

Next to the magnifying glass, we click and type the name or last name of the person we're looking for.

We won't see this point now since we have a specific chapter for every kind of search we can perform, which is one of the most powerful tools LinkedIn offers us.

4.2.4 Sending messages

When we're in the Level 1 contacts screen, on each contact's right, we have a button that consists of three grey dots.

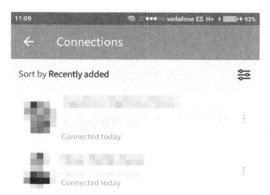

If we click that button, the option to message that contact will drop down.

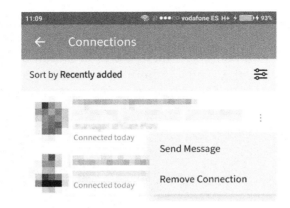

4.2.5 Eliminating contacts

On the contacts screen, when we click the three grey dots button, the menu you saw on the point above appears. By clicking on "Remove Connection" it will ask us if we're sure we want to remove this contact from our agenda.

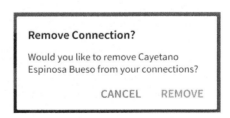

If we click "REMOVE", we'll eliminate this person from our agenda, but they won't get any notification.

4.2.6 Syncing contacts automatically

One of the possibilities the LinkedIn app grants us is indicating it we want it to automatically sync our Smartphone contacts and to let us know when a new contact signs up to LinkedIn.

On the Smartphone app main screen, we have our picture on the top right corner, we click on it.

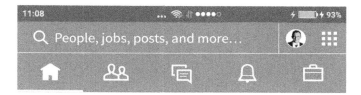

It'll take us to our Profile. On the top right we have a gear, which we have to click to go to the settings screen.

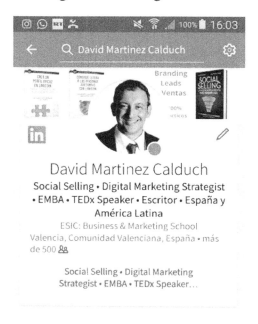

And we enter this screen:

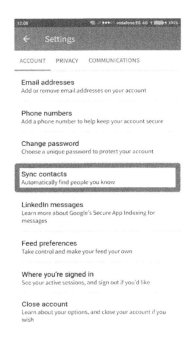

And we have an option called "Sync contacts", we click it and it'll show us two options:

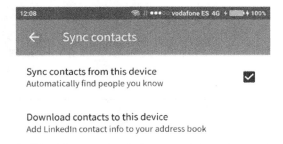

"Sync contacts from this device" is for when we want it to sync the contacts in our Smartphone to check if they're in LinkedIn, and from that moment on, to notify us if any user that we know signs up on LinkedIn. If the option is deactivated, when you activate it it'll start the process we've already seen of telling you which people you know are already on LinkedIn, and who you'd like to invite.

4.2.7 Downloading LinkedIn contacts

Following the same steps on the previous point, instead of selecting "Sync contacts from this device", now we select "Download contacts to this device", and these options will appear:

Be very careful with this option, because if you activate the first option it will download every LinkedIn contact, in my case it would be 10,000 contacts, to your Smartphone agenda.

In my case, I have the second option activated, to only sync the data of the contacts I have in my Smartphone with LinkedIn, and the last option is no kind of synchronization at all.

4.3 Syncing the Calendar

This option is for LinkedIn to notify us when we have meetings with contacts. It notifies us by showing us the profile of the person we're going to meet, so we can check their profile before the meeting.

4.3.1 Computer

You've already seen this in the 4.1.8 section "Managing sources and synchronization"

4.3.2 Android Smartphone

To set it up in Android we must follow these steps. We open the Smartphone, we go to settings, the apps section, and we select LinkedIn.

Now we go to permissions and we activate the calendar option.

Once this change is done, we open the LinkedIn app, you click on your own picture, and then in the settings icon on the top right corner of the screen; the sync calendar option will be available.

4.3.3 iOS Smartphone

We enter the contacts management screen, and on the top right of the screen we click the icon with the person and the + sign.

This screen will appear and we click the second option, "Sync calendar".

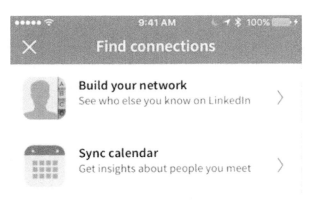

This screen will appear where we only have to activate the button.

Sync calendar

Now you must go to your iOS privacy configuration, and within Calendar, search for LinkedIn and grant it permission to access the Calendar.

4.3 Managing with a Premium account

This is the data screen that was below the main presentation card in the profiles of people we were our Level 1 contacts.

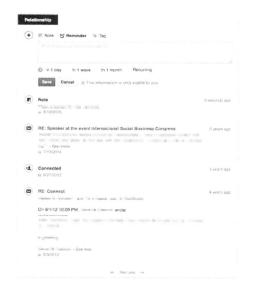

As you can see, we could label, add reminders for upcoming actions, take notes, knowing the date where we connected with them, etc. Not a CRM, but a very powerful manager.

All of it is now gone, even for paying users.

4.4 SSI - Social Selling Index

One of the tools LinkedIn provides us is an index to measure the effectiveness of our actions in LinkedIn; it'll come great to check it every month or fortnight, but don't obsess over it by visiting it everyday ;-)

https://www.linkedin.com/sales/ssi

Through some calculations, it gives us an index to measure our effectiveness. In my case, it gave me a 94 out of 100.

On the top right section, it shows two values:

- Industry SSI ranking, it means your position within the rest of professionals in your sector.

- Network SSI ranking, here it means your Level 1 contacts network, in my case the 10,000 contacts I have; the position you're in among them.

Panel sobre las ventas con redes sociales   Comparte tu SSI ⤢

David Martinez Calduch
Digital Business Transformation • Sales
C Level • Social Selling • Strategist in
Marketing Digital

1 % más alto
Clasificación SSI del sector

1 % más alto
Clasificación SSI de la red

Below, it shows us the final value, 94, and on the right it breaks down that number in four parameters it measures.

These four areas are:

1. Establish your personal brand.

2. Find the right people.

3. Interact by offering information.

4. Develop relationships.

We saw the first point in the previous book, we'll see points 2 and 4 here, and point 3 is in this Social Selling book: http://amzn.to/2tquxtx

With this, you have the four areas covered.

Further below, it shows us more information with a graph of your evolution, and below everything, what your sector SSI is, in my case it's 28, and what's the average SSI in my contacts network, which is 47.

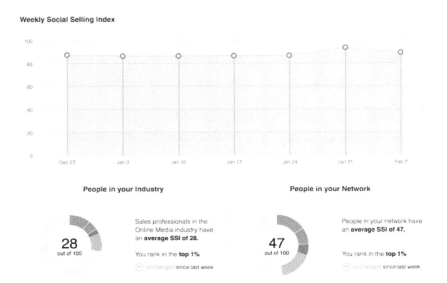

This is very useful information for us to see if we're over or under our sector or our contacts' average, and being able to see the value LinkedIn gives to the actions we're developing on real time.

Chapter 5

Messaging

"The important thing is not what's said, but how it's said."

– Cicero, philosopher from the ancient Rome

Linkedln messaging is another of the great functions it offers. How does it sound to be able to message other professionals without needing to have their email or phone number? Well, that's what LinkedIn offers us.

If this wasn't already good enough, you'll also find that when you email a person these days, they don't always respond. Instead, messages that are sent through LinkedIn have a high response ratio.

5.1 The potential of LinkedIn messaging

When you're connected with another Level 1 contact, without knowing their phone number or their email, you can message them through LinkedIn.

58% of LinkedIn users use LinkedIn messaging from their Smartphones.[2]

When well used, this tool has a great potential. When used poorly, let me tell you it'll close a lot of doors.

Remember that LinkedIn is a professional environment, where people don't have a lot of time at their disposal, and the last thing they want is someone to waste their time. So we need to know what we want to achieve and how to communicate it, in a professional and effective way.

5.2 Messaging from a computer

Now we're going to see how to use messaging from a computer.

5.2.1 Five ways to send a message

5.2.1.1 From LinkedIn screen

Regardless of which LinkedIn screen we're in, the possibility of starting a new conversation will always be available in the bottom right corner of the screen.

---

[2] Source: expandedramblings.com May-2017

There, we have three icons we're going to see how they work. The first icon is a sheet with a pencil, and clicking it will open a new window to start a conversation (only with your direct Level 1 contacts).

Now, on the top of the new window, you'll see it says "Type a name or multiple names", and here's where we type the name of the person we wish to speak to.

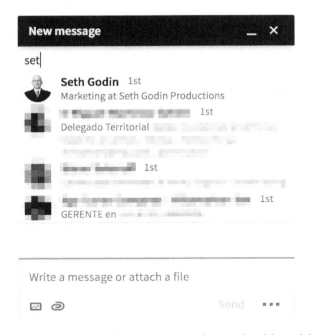

As we type, our Level 1 contacts that coincide with the text gradually appear; we click on the person we wish to speak with, and their name will appear above. Now we can message them.

If we click the second icon, the gear, we'll have the option to auto-minimize new conversations.

And the third icon, a dash, a list of the latest people we've talked with will appear.

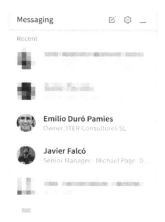

If click any of them, a new window with their name will open so we can continue talking.

You can see their picture on the right. On the bottom line we see "Read" and the other person's picture, which means the person has read the message.

5.2.1.2 From the Profile

When we enter a contact's profile, we have the option to message them below their bio, only in case they're our Level 1 contact.

Ash Maurya
Author of Running Lean and Creator of Lean Canvas.
LeanStack • Rochester Institute of Technology
Austin, Texas • 500+ ⚋

Clicking the "Message" button will open a window on the bottom right corner of the browser screen so we can start a conversation.

5.2.1.3 From the contacts screen

When we're on the contacts screen

https://www.linkedin.com/mynetwork/invite-connect/connections/

On each contact's right, we have the "Message" button. When we click it, a new conversation window will open on the bottom right corner of the browser screen.

5.2.1.4 From the messaging screen

Up on the main menu we have specific icon for Messaging.

When we click it, it'll take us to the screen from where we can manage all of our conversations, create new ones, eliminate them, etc.

On the left, we have the latest conversations list, and you'll see the last line of the conversation under each person's name.

You can see on the left that the first person is selected (highlighted in blue), so we see the conversation with them on the right side.

You'll see the word "Read" and the person's photo in the middle of the conversation, but not on the end of it. This means the messages after the "Read" are still pending to be read by the other person. In the bottom, we have the box to type and continue the conversation.

To create a new conversation, we only have to click the blue icon you can see in the image.

Messaging

We type the name of the person we wish to speak to, and we can message them by clicking their name.

5.2.1.5 From a post

On summer 2017, linked added a new feature where a box appears if we place the pointer on a person's name. This box has a message button (if they're a Level 1 contact)

5.2.2 Four kinds of content we can send

5.2.2.1 Text

To type, all we need to do is click on the typing area, and once we've finished typing, we click the "Send" button, which is in the bottom right corner.

5.2.2.2 Photos

At the bottom left corner of the messaging box we have an icon resembling an image. By clicking it, it'll open a browse window to find photos in our computer and select the one we want to send.

Once the picture is uploaded, we can include text and we click "Send". We'll see it like this.

 The maximum file size to send is 20MB.

 Allowed formats are: gif, jpeg, jpg, png, bmp.

5.2.2.3 Videos

LinkedIn now allows the native posting of videos. For now, this function is only activated from the Smartphones apps for Android and iOS.

To post videos from a computer, momentarily, you must do it via URL.

5.2.2.4 PDFs and documents

The second icon from the left is a clip icon. When we click it, a window with a file browser will appear, so we can locate and select the document we want to send.

When we click "Send" it'll look like this.

 The maximum file size to send is 20MB.

 Allowed formats are: csv, xls, xlsx, doc, docx, ppt, pptx, pdf, txt, html, htm.

5.2.2.5 URLs

We can send URLs within the text we type.

And when you click the "Send" button, you'll see the link is clickable.

5.2.3 Eliminating conversations

If we wish, we can delete a conversation, but the other person will still have it regardless; we can only delete it from our screen.

If we place the pointer on the person's name, two icons appear, and the one in the right is a trash bin. If we click it, we can delete the conversation.

Delete conversation

Sure you want to delete your entire
conversation history with Perry van Beek?

Cancel   Yes, delete

When we click it, this box will appear to confirm if we want to delete the conversation. Keep in mind this can't be undone.

Another way of doing it is with the three dots icon we have on the upper right corner of the conversation.

When we click this icon, the person's card will appear showing these options, and the third option is deleting the conversation.

5.2.4 Mark as unread

Marking a conversation as unread can come in handy to differentiate it from other conversations. For example, we might have a response pending for them, you need to send them an attachment, check something they've sent, etc. and it's easier to manage or locate it among the other conversations. It'll also make it easier to locate it when we see how to filter conversations.

When we're in the conversations screen, placing the pointer on one of the conversations on the left, two icons appear, and if we click the closed envelope icon it will mark the conversation as unread. It'll look like this now.

The bolded color looks the same as when you see unread mails.

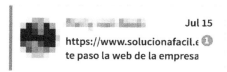

Another way of doing it is with the icon with the three dots.

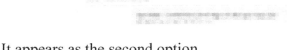

It appears as the second option.

5.2.5 Muting a conversation

With this option we're able to mute a conversation. Even if they further message us, we won't get any notification in the computer or Smartphone.

This option is also interesting when we see how to create group conversations, or in the presentations we do with various people, to minimize conversation noise.

We click on the three dots icon.

And it's the first option that appears.

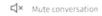

5.2.6 Searching within conversations

On the top left of the window we have the search bar within conversations.

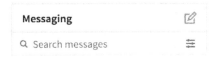

The text we type will be useful for looking:

- The conversation we've had with a person, searching their name or last name.

- Locating a conversation, searching for a word among the messages you've sent and received.

On the left figure, we see an example of finding a person named "Jaime"; we can also type a last name.

On the right figure, we have an example of a search with the term "contract", searched among the texts of the conversations.

The text you type will be search among names, last names, and the conversation.

5.2.7 Changing the conversations view

Next to the search bar we have an icon that allows us to define which conversations we want to see if we click it.

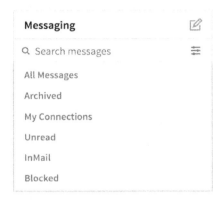

- All Messages: it's the default option.

- Archived: we can see the conversations we have archived and don't show by default. Currently, the "Archive" button has disappeared, and it's pending to be included again.

- My Connections: messages from your contacts.

- Unread: to see the messages we've marked as unread and appear in bold.

- InMail: it's a way of messaging using a Premium account, which we can use to message any LinkedIn user, regardless of the degree of separation we have, even Level 3 and outside your network.

- Blocked: the messages LinkedIn systems deem as possibly spam and are blocked. It's currently not possible to answer these messages. As I've told you before, LinkedIn is working to avoid bad practices and spam.

5.2.8 Creating a group conversation

LinkedIn messaging system also gives us the option of adding several people to create a group conversation.

We go to the conversation screen, we click the blue icon to create a new conversation.

And we type the name of the first person whom we wish to add, followed by the next person, until you've added all the people that need to be in the conversation.

We can see how it shows us the names of the people we've added on top of the box, and also tells us there're 3 people in the conversation, me and the other 2 people I added.

Now we can start the conversation and the three of us can chat. If we click the three dots icon on the top right, it'll show us the following configuration screen:

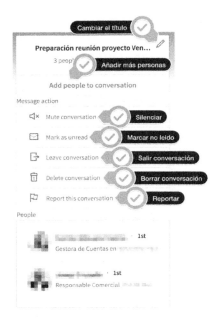

We can:

- Change the conversation title so it appears instead of the people's names.

- Add more people to the conversation, with the option of them being able to see what has been spoken until that moment, or only from the moment they're added.

- Mute the conversation so we're not notified of new messages.

- Mark this conversation as unread.

- Exit the conversation and leaving the rest of the people in it.

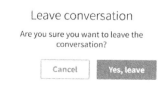

- Delete the conversation.

Sure you want to delete this?

You'll delete the entire conversation history
and won't be able to get it back.

Cancel   Yes, delete

- Report the conversation; communicate something inappropriate is happening in this conversation or with the people that are in it.

- o If we choose the third option "I think it's something else" will lead us to this screen

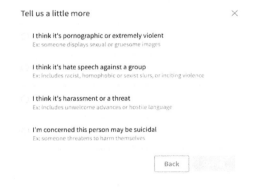

- o Pornographic or extremely violent content

- o Racism

- o Harassment or threats

- o Concern about suicidal thoughts

- And then we have the list of people who are in the conversation.

 Don't create group conversations and add people indiscriminately to advertise. This is intrusive, spam, and wasting people's time, and as you can see, you can be penalized.

Only add people you need to discuss a topic with, and it's necessary that they participate or are aware of the conversation thread.

5.2.9 Introducing people

As you saw on the previous point, doing group conversations is very interesting, but now we're going to see it from a different point of view.

One of the uses I give it is to introduce people.

Imagine we have two people who are both our Level 1 contacts, but don't know each other.

We can create a conversation adding there 2 people and introduce them. Even if they're each other's Level 2 contacts and theoretically can't talk to each other, by placing them both in the same group conversation they can talk.

5.3 Global messaging from the computer

LinkedIn latest version has now enables access to messaging in a simpler way, with the option we have on the top menu at our disposal, and also in the bottom right with the messages with alerts.

First you'll see a green dot, which means we are connected.

5.3.1 Activity status

A new feature LinkedIn has provided for messaging is being able to indicate if we want our Level 1 contacts to know if we're currently in LinkedIn or not.

To activate or deactivate it, we must go to the top menu, click on the "Me" with an arrow pointing down (under your photo), and select "Settings & Privacy".

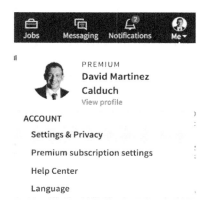

When we enter we'll get to this screen we see next; you can also get there directly through this URL in the computer.

https://www.linkedin.com/psettings/presence?trk=li_corpblog_active_status_messaging

or this one http://ow.ly/jBmj30eEcvP

Another way of getting there is entering the configuration of this new messaging screen.

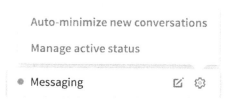

We click the wheel at the right and we click "Manage active status".

When we get to the security screen, we enter the core menu "Privacy", and on the left, we click "Profile privacy", and these options will appear on the center:

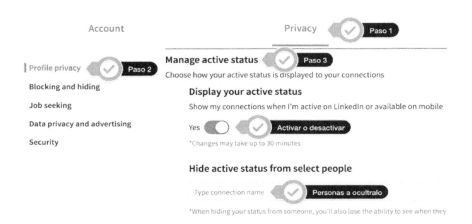

In "Display your active status" we can activate or deactivate the visibility of our state. We can also leave it activated and enter the names of certain people we want to keep our status hidden from.

This activity status will appear wherever our profile pic appears, for example, when we visit our profile.

We'll also see it on the messaging status.

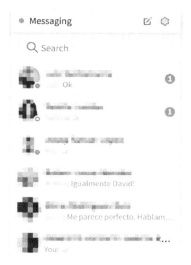

You can see the first and third person have the icon completely green; they're online, and the second one has it green with a white fill. They have their status active, but aren't currently online.

The rest of the people don't have the dot because they haven't activated this option.

5.3.2 Alerts

The advantage of this window is that we quickly can see how many new messages we have.

You can see the whole window becomes dark, and it indicates us how many new messages we have with a red background.

5.3.3 Messages

To open and close this messaging window, all we need to do is click on "Messaging" or the number.

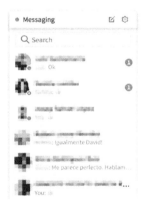

5.3.4 Writing a new message

To open and close this messaging window, all we need to do is click on "Messaging" or the number.

5.3.5 Configuration

If we click the wheel on the right, two options will appear.

Auto-minimize new conversations.

Manage active status, which will lead us to the status configuration screen, to toggle if we want it visible or not.

5.4 Messaging from a Smartphone

We also have this fabulous communication tool from Smartphones, which also includes some features that are only available for Smartphones that we're going to check.

5.4.1 Three places where to send a message

5.4.1.1 From the contacts manager

When we're in the contacts screen, which we can get to by tapping the contacts icon.

And then we click the number that appears on the left, which is the amount of contacts we have.

Our contacts list will appear, and on each contact's right, each one has a three dots icon, and if we click it we can message them.

5.4.1.2 From the Profile

If we enter the profile of one of our Level 1 contacts, we have the "Message" button.

The conversation screen is the same as in the computer.

5.4.1.3 From the messaging screen

On top of the main menu, we have a specific icon for Messaging.

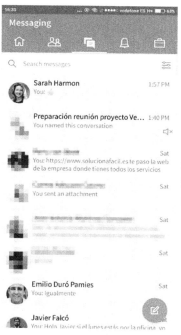

When we click it, it takes us to the screen where we have all of our conversations.

On the bottom right, we have a blue round button with a sheet and pencil inside. If we click it, it'll take us to the screen we'll see next.

And we write the name of the person we're looking for.

At each person's right, we have a circle to select them to chat.

5.4.2 Seven kinds of content we can send

5.4.2.1 Text

We just have to click the area that says "Type a message" and write. To send the written message, we have round button with an arrow.

5.4.2.2 Photos

In the message typing area, we have a button resembling a camera.

When we click it, it sows these two options: taking a photo directly from the camera, or selecting a photo from our Smartphone gallery.

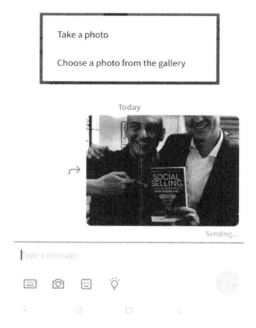

As you can see, the photo appears decreased. To see its full size, you have to click it.

5.4.2.3 Photo Galleries

A new feature LinkedIn has launched on summer 2017 is the possibility of posting a gallery with multiple photos

From the Smartphone app, we click the button for posting photos from the gallery and we select the photos we want to post.

By clicking the "Done" button on the upper right corner, it'll show us a preview of how it'll look and now we can write the text we want to post.

And then we click "Post".

This kind of post is great for showing several pictures of an event, different views of our offices, combinations of products from various points of view, etc.

5.4.2.4 Videos

LinkedIn has activated the native posting of videos. To be able to post videos, we have to do it from the Smartphone app.

We click the Posting icon.

In the Post screen, on the bottom we see we have the video camera icon.

When we click it, two options appear: we can publish a video from our gallery, or we can record one live.

Android   iOS

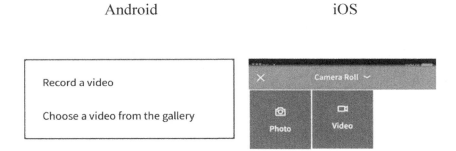

And this is how it looks.

5.4.2.5 PDFs and documents

In the current version of the LinkedIn app, you can't send documents.

5.4.2.6 URLs

Works exactly as in the computer.

5.4.2.7 Emoticons

LinkedIn app allows us to send emoticons that are already in the app. There are two galleries; to activate them, we click this icon:

You'll see eight images.   You can swipe for more.

You can notice another gallery on the button. As you can see, it's a cup of coffee. If we click it, the gallery will load.

Eight images appear.   And, same as before, you can
                                                swipe for more.

To post one, you must click it to select it, and it'll appear like this.

As a safety measure to confirm we want to publish it, if we click on the upper left, we have an X to cancel the post, and if we do want to post it, we click the image we see again.

5.4.2.8 Animated Gifs

Besides, we can upload animated gifs from other galleries. We have a + sign on the right.

When we click it, this screen appears.

If you click the + signs on the right, you'll download the galleries.

If you swipe, there are more below.

Once they're loaded, they'll appear at the bottom, below the typing box.

To use them, we just need to click the one we want to use and let the images load. Remember you can swipe up to see the rest of the gallery.

The work the same as we saw before: we click the image, a previsualization appears, and we can see the gif animation.

5.4.3 Eliminating conversations

To eliminate a conversation with a person or several people, we must click on the upper right, where names of the person or people who are in the conversation appear.

And the last option in the screen that appears is deleting the conversation.

When we click "DELETE CONVERSATION" a confirmation message will appear.

5.4.4 Marking as unread

On the conversations list, if we tap and hold, this screen appears.

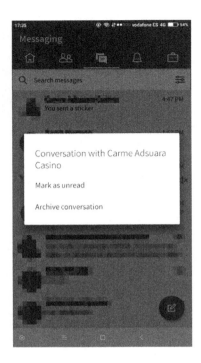

5.4.5 Muting a conversation

To mute a conversation, we enter it and, on the top right, we click the photo.

We have the "Mute" option on the screen that appears.

5.4.6 Searching within conversations

When we're in the Messaging screen, we have an area that says "Search messages" where we can type the text we wish to search.

It works the same as in the computer.

5.4.7 Archiving conversations

To archive a conversation, from the conversations list, we tap and hold until this screen appears:

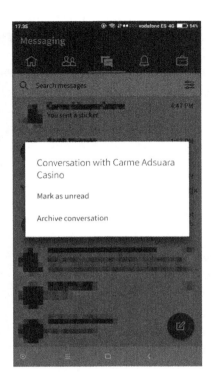

Another way of archiving conversations is entering the conversation, clicking the photo on the top right.

And clicking the "Archive" button on the screen that appears.

ARCHIVE

5.4.8 Creating a group conversation

As we saw before, we have to click the icon with a sheet and a pencil to create a conversation from the Messaging screen.

Searching for the person we wish to chat with, we can directly select several people. We conduct a search, and we select one; we make a new search, and we select another, and that's how we place them together in the same conversation.

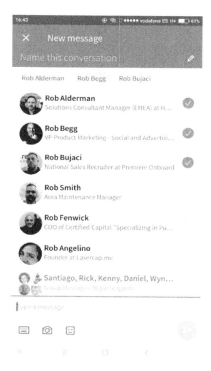

When we're in the conversation, to be able to access the options, we must click the top right, where the photos of the people that are in the conversation are shown.

We can:

- Change the conversation title.

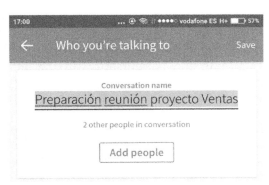

- Add more people to the conversation and indicate if we want them to see what has been written so far.

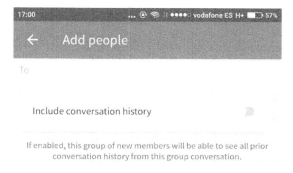

- Mute the conversation so we don't get notifications of new messages.

- Archive the conversation; save it, so it doesn't appear on the list.

- Leave the conversation and leave the rest of the people in it.

- See the list of people in the conversation.

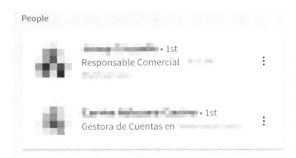

- o And if we click the three grey dots icon on the right, these two options appear.

- o The first option is to send a direct message outside the group conversation.

- o And the second one is to report some kind of inappropriate behavior.

- o Same as in the computer, if you select the second option, more options appear.

- Delete the conversation, which is the last option that appears.

DELETE CONVERSATION

5.4.9 Introducing people

The same way we've introduced people in the computer, we can do from the Smartphone, they work the same way.

5.5 InMail messages

InMail messages are messages we can send to any person who's signed up on LinkedIn, regardless of them being our Level 2, Level 3, or out of our network, literally allowing us to contact any person in LinkedIn (remember there is a Damocles' Sword).

With the different Premium versions of LinkedIn, we have access to send a determined amount of InMail messages. This amount of InMails we have available is determined by several factors:

1. Depending on the Premium version hired, we have between 3 and 150 InMail messages per month

    a. Business: 3 to 5

    b. Premium Business: 10 to 15

    c. Executive: 25 to 30

    d. Sales Navigator Basic: 5 to 8

    e. Sales Navigator Pro: 10 to 15

    f. Sales Navigator Team: 25 to 30

    g. Recruiter Lite: 25 to 30

    h. Recruiter Professional Services: 50 to 100

    i. Recruiter Corporate: 50 to 150

2. InMails we send to other people who are also Premium users like us are free and aren't discounted.

3. For every InMail someone answers in a 90 days term from the date of issue, you'll get another one when the recipient responds or when they check the "not interested" option.

4. You'll receive the credit when the recipient responds.

5. InMails we don't use are accumulated for the next months. They can remained unused for 90 days maximum.

6. InMail messages we withdraw can't be recovered.

Remember that the messages you send with InMail are a reflection of your company and your personal brand.

Be brief and go straight to the point.

- LinkedIn, InMail use

The title size can be of up to 200 characters, and the message body can be of up to 2,000 characters.

Use InMail messages to start a conversation, don't try to seal an agreement. It's the beginning of a conversation and a way to explore possibilities.

Comment and mention what caught your attention in their profile, what made you contact them.

The best tone is a familiar and enthusiastic tone, but be natural, you must use the words that reflect the way you talk.

LinkedIn is a site for making friends, not a bulletin board.

Job searching:

Show an honest interest in helping them achieve their objectives, instead of your need to get the position.

A new contact opportunity today could result in many candidates in the future.

Don't copy and paste the job description or the URL in the job ad.

Recruiters:

As an expert in selection, you have a personal brand, so you need to take care of your professional image, since candidates will perceive you as a trusted speaker.

If you share too much information, it'll make the candidates not see the need of responding the message.

Focus in finding out their availability and interest for the job.

Candidates that aren't actively looking for a job won't respond the "check this job ad and tell me if you're interested" kind of message.

It's better to start the conversation by asking about their careers and professional objectives.

Encourage them to respond by asking them for advice, opinions, and references.

Studies have proved that using the person's name while you speak to them improves their impression of us, and increases the possibility of effectiveness in communication.

5.5.1 Sending InMails

To send an InMail, we go to the profile of a person who isn't our Level 1 contact, and the option of sending them an InMail and trying to connect with that person will appear.

In this case, it was a Level 2 contact and it gave us the possibility of connecting; when they're a Level 3 or out of our network, it can appear in two different ways.

In this way of showing it, you have to click on "More..." so the menu drops down, and you have the InMail option

The other way you can find is this one, where you already have the InMail button directly.

To send an InMail, we click the button and this screen will appear.

Unlike messaging, here we do have the "Subject", and we can write the message below. In the bottom right you'll see that it indicates us we have 10 InMails left to use this month.

5.5.2 Managing InMails

To manage sent InMails we must go to the messaging screen, where we have the InMail option among the filters by types of messages.

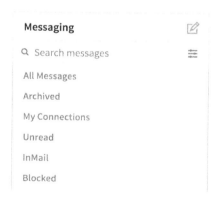

To manage sent InMails we must go to the messaging screen, where we have the InMail option among the filters by types of messages. When we select it, a list of all the InMails we've sent and received will appear.

When we open one we've sent, we'll see if it has been answered or not. In this case, it hasn't.

In case they respond, it works the same as we saw in messaging.

On the top right corner of the conversation we have a button with three dots.

And when we click it, this options about the person who sent us the InMail appear.

Muting the conversation, mark the conversation as unread, deleting the conversation, and reporting the conversation for inappropriate use.

5.5.3 Marking an InMail as unread

In the conversations list, when we place the pointer on one of them, two icons appear: the closed envelope icon is to mark it as unread.

5.5.4 Erasing InMails

In the same screen as before, when we place the pointer on the InMail, we also have the trash bin icon, and if we click it, we delete the message.

Remember this can't be undone, and the old deleted messages bin no longer exists, momentarily.

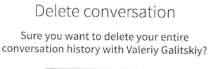

5.5.5 Responding InMails

Selecting one of the received InMails, we see the message that was sent to us and, below everything, we can write our response. Three buttons with pre-written responses appear by default, if we click any of them, the prewritten response appears on the typing field and we can modify it, so it's easier and quicker to respond.

To manage sent InMails we must go to the messaging screen where we can we can filter messages by type. Among those types, there's the InMail option.

5.5.6 InMails from a Smartphone

We enter the messaging menu and we click the "Search message" icon on the right, and the options will roll out.

We click "InMail", and now we have access to all our InMail messages. We can respond, but we can't create new InMail messages.

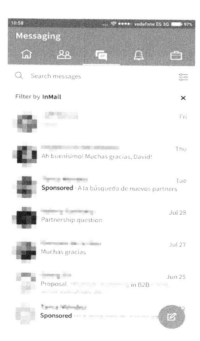

5.6 How to make messaging work

"The only way of winning is learning faster than anybody else"

- Eric Ries, author of The Lean Startup

One of the great challenges you'll face is how is it possible to create messages that achieve the objective we chase: getting a response, arranging a meeting, catching the person's interest on the topic we're bringing up.

The best advice I can give you is to use the Lean Startup methodology: Create – Measure – Learn. You must define a text for each kind of objective / product / service and test it, make small changes, and see exactly which one gives you the best results.

Let's see the structure of an effective message.

1. Title

2. Customized greeting with the person's name

3. Who you are, name and company

4. What we have in common

5. Something we've observed about that person

6. Value contribution

Bonus:

7. Question

8. Raising interest

9. Petition

10. Closure and thanks

To make sure we have positive response rate, the first thing we need to do is informing ourselves about the person we're about to contact.

5.6.1 Title

It's important that the first phrase we send, the old title, is as clear and concrete as possible, so the person who receives it knows what we want.

35% of open emails remain like that due to their subject.

- Aaron Kahlow, CEO at Online Marketing Institute

You must keep in mind that the title is the only thing the person receiving the message will see. They'll only see the rest of the message when they click it.

The title's length is also important since, as you can see in the image, they can only see a part of the first text you send.

How it looks on a computer:

How it looks on a Smartphone, where it shows a little more text.

The title I speak about here, with LinkedIn's new Messaging function, has been rendered nearly useless. It makes more sense to use it for InMail messaging.

5.6.2 Customized greeting with the person's name

Politeness above all. The least we can do is writing "Hello" and their name; this will show that we at least cared enough to know what their name is, and we'll clear doubts about this being written by a person instead of being an automated message.

5.6.3 Who you are, name and company

We must help the person we're messaging know who we are and in which company.

If we don't do it, the person receiving the message has to start researching who you are, what you do, and what your company is. Don't you think this will affect our effectiveness? We're giving them extra work and we're deviating them from our objective, which is for them to focus on the rest of the message.

5.6.4 What we have in common

When we name people we have in common, response rates are higher. This is because we create a common bond that builds confidence, and it brings the possibility of asking someone they know about you.

We can also indicate if we have these in common:

- Groups. Search among the debates so you can comment about them in the message, it's a good way of breaking

You have 21% higher probability of receiving a response from a candidate if you send an InMail message to someone you share a group with.

- LinkedIn, for recruiters

- University, Business School, or even high school

- Previous companies

Mentioning a company in common increases the possibility of receiving a response to an InMail message in 27%.

- LinkedIn

- The same industry

- Coworkers or former coworkers

- Country or region of origin

- Followers of your company

People who follow your company on LinkedIn are 81% more inclined to respond to your InMail messages than those who don't. Use the «Company followers» filter to find these people.

- LinkedIn

- Company in common

Mentioning a company in common increases the possibility of receiving a response to an InMail message in 27%.

- LinkedIn

- Education in common (you'll see this with the Schools searcher)

- Interests in common (by checking their profile)

5.6.5 Something we've observed about this person

Before we message someone, it might be a good idea to see this person's activity before by visiting their profile, where we can see their posts, group interactions, etc. being able to see if we're interested in giving our opinion about something they've commented (always positive, not critic in any case, much less entering in polemic grounds –politics, religion, etc.-), or not saying anything but keeping it in mind when sending the message.

We can also make a comment regarding something we've seen in their profile, functions, specialties, languages, etc.

The same way as when we speak on the phone, if you have a smile on your face, the other person notices. If you're honest or not when writing your message, have no doubt they will be able to notice it.

5.6.6 Value contribution

Can we grant something of value in the conversation?

- We have current information on something they commented

- We have data on their industry nobody else has

- We've seen something in which we can advise them

- You know someone they could use, because you saw them commenting they were looking for something

What we contribute must be without offense or trying to look smart or superior, but a humble and selfless value contribution instead. And it also has to be true; if you don't feel like it, it's better you don't do it.

If you noticed they made a mistake, or they're wrong about something, NEVER point it out in public. Do you like to be ridiculed in public? Or corrected in public?

It's better to privately message them. Once sent, it's their decision if they fix it or not. If they're stubborn about not acknowledging their mistake, you politely greet them and step away before you get in trouble and your good intentions harm you. We're not looking for confrontations, we're looking to create communication bridges, and we'll hardly achieve that by arguing.

5.6.7 Three kinds of questions

There's nothing better for knowing something than asking.

> *"There are no questions without answers, only poorly formulated questions."*
>
> *- Matrix*

Starting a conversation by asking a questions gets good results.

- "Do you have any doubt about [topic] you wish to solve?"

- "Is [topic] among your priorities?"

- "Are you contemplating [topic] during this year?"

5.6.7.1 Open questions

Other kinds of questions we can make are open questions, which are questions that don't look for a yes or a no; instead, the people can write anything they want, and if it's about themselves, who doesn't like speaking about themselves? ;-) These kinds of questions can start with:

- Who, when, what, why, where and how

- A few examples:

- "Which kinds of […] do you prefer?"

- "What are your marked goals for this year?"

- "In which projects are you currently involved?"

5.6.7.2 Closed questions

Another type of questions are closed questions. The objective here is to obtain a more concrete answers, and we start those questions with:

- Do, have and be

A few examples:

- "Do you like […]?"

- "Have you ever been to […]?"

- "Do you know […]?"

"When we thought we had all the answers, suddenly, they changed all the questions"

- Mario Benedetti

Uruguayan writer, poet and playwright

5.6.7.3 Combined questions

We can also make combinations, where we make an observation and we throw an open question.

- "That's a good [topic], where did you find that information?"

- "I saw the post you made, how do you think [topic] will evolve?"

- "You really generated a lot of noise and comments, some of them very strong, which one do you believe is most on target?"

- "I'm also going to the conference, which lecture do you believe is most powerful?"

- "Have you seen the news on [company, sector, etc.]? I really believe [your opinion]. What do you believe?"

5.6.8 Good and bad topics to discuss

5.6.8.1 Topics to discuss

Here are some topics that can be good to start a conversation:

- About the company's own blog/website (the other person's company)

- A new app in the industry

- About a conference, lecture, or lecturer

5.6.8.2 Topics you shouldn't discuss

It's better not to touch certain topics to avoid dangerous conversations:

- Politics

- Religion

- Feminism, etc.

- Criticizing anyone

- The weather. Are you seriously asking about the weather? :-0

5.6.9 Raising interest

Show an honest interest about something you wish to know or learn, and raise it to the other person. Sincerity can be noted, it's transferred via electric waves and it reaches the other person.

5.6.10 Making a petition

To conclude, you can suggest to have coffee to de-virtualize each other, or you can also schedule a Skype call. But keep in mind that...

"Asking for an appointment kills response rates in 90% - 97%"

- Sharon Drew Morgen, Developer Change Facilitation

This data makes reference to when we're in the selling process. If we're on the contacting process, acceptance rates are quite high; it always depends on their availability and their work load.

5.6.11 Closure and thanks

The final two lines are very important, because that's where we seal all the work we've done on the messages.

We're going to encourage our interlocutor to respond the message in a polite and educated manner.

"Thank you for your time and I'm looking forward to your feedback. Regards".

Selling mode – You must remember that our goal is not to sell, this won't work, but to initiate a conversation. Going straight to selling makes response rates minimal.

5.6.12 When to message

The best days to message and have a bigger effectiveness are Tuesdays, Wednesdays, or Thursdays, in the morning. The reason is that Mondays is when the week starts, and everyone is quite busy, and Fridays is when it ends, before the weekend starts.

Messaging early in the morning is better, since they can see it even before they get to work or when they just got there, before they begin with all the day's tasks.

5.7 Messages for Recruiters

Messaging is very useful, but if we're Recruiters, we have to be capable of reaching every possible candidate, with no limitation to which Level they're in, so InMail is the solution we're looking for.

On average, LinkedIn Recruiter users send almost a million InMail messages to LinkedIn members every week. - LinkedIn

5.7.1 Most common mistakes to avoid and advice

Don't think about yourself, focus on the candidate.

In the first message, don't ask for the resume, nor names of other people who may be interested in the position.

Value their achievements, and ask them about their interests and professional objectives. Analyze if they have the right profile before you ask them for their resume or to fill up their application.

In order for the candidate to be more receptive to give you references of other people, you'll need time to reinforce your credibility and earn their trust.

Don't offer the candidate a lower position than the one they already have.

70% of the members who started in a new position in the last 12 months got promoted or switched to a position of the same level.

- LinkedIn

Candidates with fixed contracts don't accept temporal contracts, and if they've had several temporal contracts it's difficult they want to sign a temporal contract for several months.

Not doing things right will harm your company's reputation, and yours; things like contacting candidates whose profile and experience don't match the offered position, or not writing a personalized message.

5.7.2 When is it better to message

The weekend is not a good idea to send InMail messages. Messages sent on Saturdays are 16% less likely to be responded compared to the ones send during the midweek.

Between 9 and 10 in the morning (on the recipient's time zone) is the best time, and Thursday is the best day of the week. This time is 12% better compared to a Friday afternoon when people are already thinking about the weekend.

5.7.3 Metrics to analyze

LinkedIn recommends us a few formulas to be able to analyze our messaging performance.

Accepted InMail messages = number of messages the candidates respond to by clicking **Reply to this message**

Rejected InMail messages = number of messages the candidates respond to by clicking **Not interested**, whichever the motive

Pending InMail messages (no response) = number of messages the candidates haven't responded to

Total InMail messages = accepted messages + rejected messages + pending messages

Acceptance index = (accepted messages) / (total messages)

Respond percentage = (accepted messages + rejected messages) / (total messages)

5.8 How to do mailing

One of the possible options we may want to use is mailing our LinkedIn contacts.

Currently, it can't be done from LinkedIn, since LinkedIn aims for one to one communications, where quality primes over quantity.

To be able to do it, we must export our contacts agenda, how we saw on point **4.1.7 Exporting contacts**.

Once we've exported our contacts' data we can use Mailchimp or Quadux Server for large volumes of emails for their low cost. https://quadux.net/send-envio-masivo-mailings/

Chapter 6

Contacts Search

*"I can teach anybody how to get what they want
out of life. The problem is that I can't find
anybody who can tell me what they want"*

- Mark Twain

One of the great and powerful tools that LinkedIn has at our disposition is its search engine, where we have a great variety of filters to be able to locate the people we're interested in reaching.

In this chapter, you're going to see the different kinds of searches there are, how to use them from a computer, and from a Smartphone.

6.1 Basic searches from a computer

On the top right of the screen, we see LinkedIn's logo with a magnifying glass next to it with the word "Search".

If we click on that text and we write what we want to look for, without clicking anything, results will show up as we write.

6.1.1 Searching for a person

This search engine LinkedIn offers to us is a global search engine that allows us to do quick searches.

Let's make our first search; we click on the box that says "Search" and we type "Michael" (without the quote marks). As you can see, you don't need to press Enter or any button; the search is automatic.

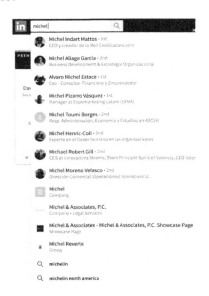

The first results are our Level 1 contacts. In this case, there's only 1.

And then our Level 2 contacts appear.

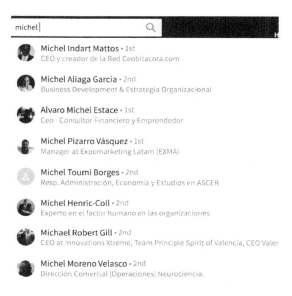

To see the Level 3 or out of network contacts we have to use advanced searches, which we'll see later. Next, there appear companies and groups with a similar name.

At the end, it proposes (in this case) a couple alternative searches, which will execute if we click them, and we'll see the results.

If we click on any person, company or group, it'll take us directly to their profile and we can investigate and interact.

This same example we've shown with the name also works with last names.

6.1.2 Searching for a position

We type "CEO" so results show.

The first result is for when we want to buy CEO job positions, the second is for finding people with a CEO position, and the third one is to find groups about CEOs.

Then, there appear people, companies, groups, universities and Showcase Page.

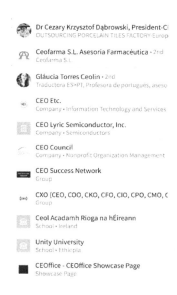

6.1.3 Searching for a skill

Imagine we're looking for an iOS developer; we type "iOS" in the query box and then we see the results.

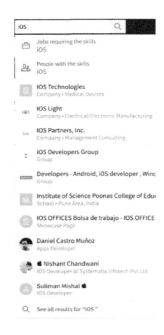

LinkedIn has detected it as a knowledge or skill and the first thing it asks us is if we want to find job positions that require "iOS", or if we're looking for people with "iOS" skills.

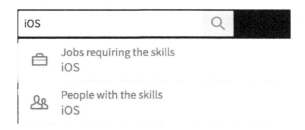

The results shown next are companies, groups, universities Showcase Page and people with that word in the name.

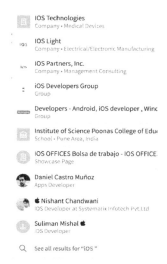

6.1.4 Searching a company

If we type the name of a company in the search box, the first thing that'll appear are the people who work in it and job offers. Let's see the "Tesla mo" example.

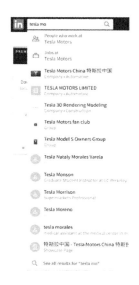

Since it detected it is a company, now the first thing that appears are two search proposals: if we want to search for employees of this company or if we want to see job offers from this company, and it's as simple as clicking the option we want to see the results.

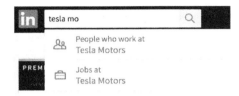

The following results it shows are company profiles and groups.

And then it shows us people with those words in their name and a search proposal.

6.1.5 Searching for a University

Now let's search for a university with this text: "University of Barcelona"

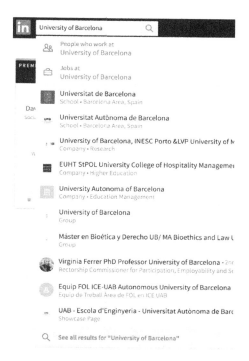

In the first results we see the same options that appear on company, people who work at the university and job offers.

The next result is universities with the same name.

Then, companies appear.

And next, groups, people (with those words in their profiles), Showcase Page[3] and at the end, a search proposal.

Let's make another search so you see how LinkedIn adapts the results to the type of search we do. Now, let's search for the word "Monterrey".

---

[3] They're additional pages that can be created in LinkedIn, hanging from the company's page, where you can show information on a range of products or services.

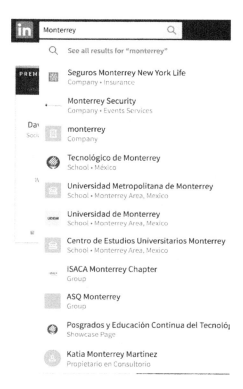

Since we didn't enter the word university, the first thing that appears are companies.

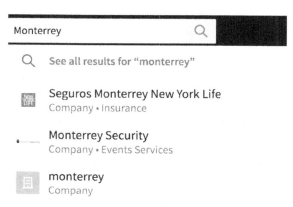

And after companies, universities show up.

And at the end we see groups, Showcase Pages and people with those words on their names.

6.1.6 Conclusions

With this global search engine we can make searches very quickly. LinkedIn tries to identify the kind of content we're looking for and adapts the proposals it makes and the results.

I use this type of search very often, since it's a very fast way to locate a person or a company. In case I don't locate them easily enough, that's when I do perform advanced searches, which we'll see later.

6.2   Basic   searches   from   a Smartphone

6.2.1 Search bar

When we open our LinkedIn app from a Smartphone, there's a box with a magnifying glass (like in a computer) at the top of the screen, and next to it, a text "People, jobs, posts, and more…"

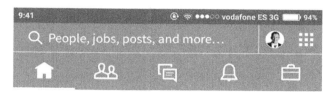

When we open our LinkedIn app from a Smartphone, there's a box with a magnifying glass (like in a computer) at the top of the screen, and next to it, a text "People, jobs, posts, and more…"

Regardless of if we click the magnifying glass or the text next to it, it'll take us to search screen.

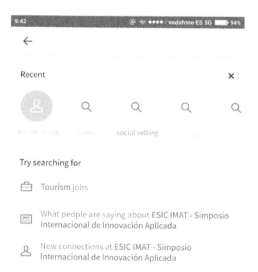

Above everything, we have the area for searches, which now we'll see how to use it to search, then we have a zone called

"Recent", where the searches we have done so far appear, both in the Smartphone and the computer; this is synchronized. If we click on any recent search, it does that search again, and if we touch and drag it to the left, it shows more results.

If you don't want to use or see "Recent" searches, there's an X at the right to disable it.

I personally like it, since I can conduct a search from the Smartphone, and when I go back to the computer I can continue from it, or the other way around. It's very practical.

Below, it shows us some searches suggestions which we can use. In my case, since I'm in the IMAT Organizing Committee, it suggests a "Tourism jobs" search, people who are commenting about IMAT in LinkedIn, and people who belong in IMAT.

Try searching for

📁 Tourism jobs

🗒 What people are saying about **ESIC IMAT - Simposio** Internacional de Innovación Aplicada

👤 New connections at **ESIC IMAT - Simposio** Internacional de Innovación Aplicada

6.2.2 Five kinds of searches

The searches' functioning is exactly the same as in a computer, you can try doing the same searches we saw.

Search for a person

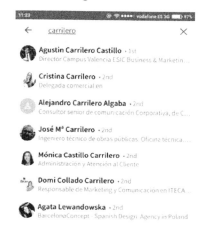

Search for a position

Search for a skill

Search for a company

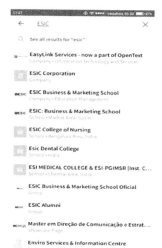

Search for a University

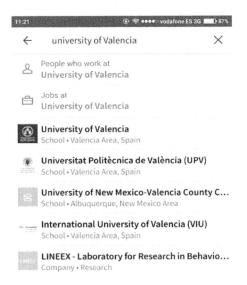

Chapter 7

Advanced Searches

One of the best tool that LinkedIn provides is its powerful search and advanced searches tool. If we use it correctly, I can assure you there are no limits when achieving our objectives.

We go back to the computer, and we're in the search box on the top left corner.

If we write the text we want to look up and press Enter, we'll go to the advanced searches screen.

If we wish to access the advanced searches screen with all the kinds of filters there are, and every kind of search, then we have to click directly on the magnifying glass icon, which will take us to this screen.

Now we're going to see the advanced searches screen structure, the different sections and what each one of them is for.

At the top left, we have the area to write the text we want to look for.

Below that, we have the kinds of searches depending on what we search.

We have the following kinds of searches:

- People, to only search for people.

- Jobs, to only search for jobs.

- Post, to look for posts made in Pulse, LinkedIn's posting platform.

- All, all kinds mixed.

- Companies, to only search for companies.

- Groups, to only search for groups.

- Schools, to "only" look for universities.

The left side is where the results appear and it indicates us the quantity, which in this case is 5,367,158 people.

Under each person, it shows their picture, name and last name, in what level they are (in this case they're all Level 1), and then their position and location. Below, there appear pictures of people we have in common and the quantity of mutual contacts.

On the right, we have the "Message" button we've already seen so we can message them.

The top right corner of the screen is where we have the filtering zone, to reduce the results and focus in the people who actually interest us.

Instead of going through every screen explaining what every button does, we're going to see it in my usual way of teaching, which is using practical real examples, and we'll see which functions we need in each case. Rest assured, for when we're done you'll have seen all of them.

7.1 Twelve ways of searching for a person

The way searches work is exactly the same as in a computer; you can try doing the same searches we saw.

Since we want to focus on finding people only, the first thing we'll do is clicking the magnifying glass to go to advanced search, and we choose "People".

7.1.1 Searching by name

One of the ways of searching by name, and it's a valid one, is writing the person's name directly on the top part, where it says "Search".

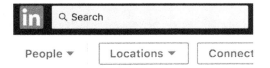

If we do it this way, it won't only search the text in their name, but also in every part of the profile. Sometimes it can be a good idea, but if we want to filter our results significantly, it's not the better choice.

We're going to do each search in its corresponding field to be able to find the most accurate results possible. In this screen we find, on the top right corner, we have an option called "All Filters".

All Filters

And this screen appears with every available filter option.

All people filters

First name	Company	Connections
		1st
Last name	School	2nd
		3rd+
Title		

Connections of	Locations	Current companies
Add connection of	Add a location	Add a company
	United States	Google
	Spain	Amazon
	India	Microsoft
	Valencia Area, Spain	LinkedIn
	United Kingdom	IBM

Past companies	Industries	Profile language
Add a company	Add an industry	English
IBM	Marketing and Advertising	Spanish
Microsoft	Information Technology and Services	French
Accenture	Human Resources	Portuguese
Google	Internet	Italian
Hewlett Packard Enterprise	Staffing and Recruiting	

Nonprofit interests	Schools
Skilled Volunteering	Add a school
Board Service	University of Valencia
	Universitat Politècnica de València (UPV)
	Universidad Complutense de Madrid
	ESIC Business & Marketing School
	Universitat de Barcelona

In this case, we're going to find people by their name. In my case, I write "Jaime" and I touch the upper right blue button that says "Apply", and it throws "Showing 240, 848 results" as result.

Cancel   **Apply**

Search with Sales Navigator

When writing "Jaime" it's the same to write it in lowercase "jaime" than in uppercase "JAIME". The same results will show.

The number that appears, which in this case is 240,848 people, depends on our contacts agenda. Do the same search yourself; the amount of people you can reach, and who they are, depends on how you've worked on your contacts agenda.

For this reason, the first part of this book was to start with the agenda, since it'll limit you when making searches and being able to reach the people you wish to reach. And if you can't, well, we have InMail.

The number it marks as people who comply with the search criteria is all the people we're able to reach in Level 1, Level 2 and Level 3.

To see the amount of contacts we have in each Level, what we do is select the concrete Level we wish to filter.

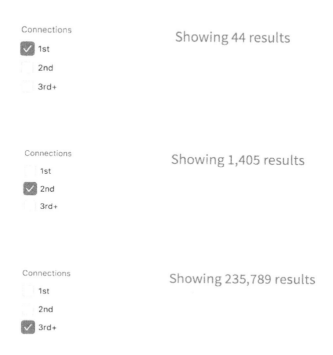

What is this good for?

Level 1, so we can search within our current contacts, with whom we're already connected and we can message.

Level 2, because we focus on people we're able to invite so they can become our Level 1.

Level 3, did you see the volume of results? That's where your clients and your next job is.

If we don't activate any of the three levels, then results from all the levels will show.

Connections

☐ 1st

☐ 2nd

☐ 3rd+

Results are always sorted by Level; all the Level 1 contacts appear first, then the Level 2, and then the Level 3.

Now we're going to do another search by name. We remove "Jaime", we write "Angels" and press Enter, and this is the result that shows.

We've searched "Angels" and you can see how the first 4 results are "Àngels", with a grave accent, and the last result is an "Angels" without the accent.

What I want to show with this is that accents in the names and last names are no longer a problem.

7.1.2 Searching by last name

Now we're going to make a search by last name, we press "All Filters" and we type "Rodriguez" in the "Last name" field

When we press Enter we see results.

Now we're going to continue the search we did before with "Jaime" and we'll add this last name. It'll look like this:

And the results shown are the following:

You can see results like "Jaime [text] Rodriguez" or "Jaime Rodriguez", and also both with accent and without.

7.1.3 Search by title or position

If you read the search in the previous point, to start a new search erasing all the filters you've done, we have in the right zone, where the filters are, the "Clear all" option.

If you click it, it'll delete all the filter you applied, in this case 2 filters, as it appears next to the word Clear.

Let's suppose we want to find people linked with the sales world, and that's the word we're going to search in "Title", I enter the text "Sales" and click the "Apply" button.

Title

Sales

You can see how it locates them both in lowercase and uppercase, and by indicating the Title filter, it searches within the Professional Title on top of the whole Professional Profile.

If we see the positions that appear, they are:

- Office manager/**Sales**

- Group **Sales** Account Executive

- Inside **Sales** Representative

- Inside **Sales** Manager

- **Sales** and Marketing

They're all "Sales", but each one of them has a position, now we want to focus the search in "Sales Manager" only, and we do this search.

Title

Sales Manager|

And these are the results that are shown.

In the first result, we have the word "manager" and "sales" separately, in the rest of results, they match exactly.

If what we want of for only "Sales Manager" to appear, we have to do it like this, placing the text between quote marks, so we force it to search for that text exactly.

Title

Now we can check that all the results have "Sales Manager" in their Title, in uppercase and lowercase.

You've probably noticed the number of results has been reduced, from a fairly generic search, until reaching the person we're interested in concretely.

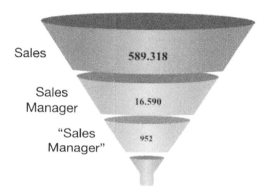

Trying to contact 589 thousand people is completely inviable, trying to do so with 16 thousand too, but 952 people starts to become a number that, if we tune in a little more, we can reduce and really reach the people we're interested in.

About this last search, now we can define, knowing what we're looking for, Sales Managers from:

- A geographic zone

- A specific industry

- A company or group

- Etc.

Like a funnel, we gradually reduce the amount so it's really manageable and useful.

7.1.4 Searching by location

Now we're going to filter by location so we can reduce our results even more.

On top of the search bar, on the left part, we click "Location" and this screen drops down.

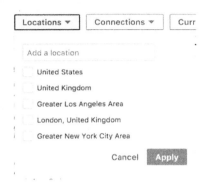

We can select countries, regions and cities. Let's select "Valencia Area, Spain" by clicking the box, and we press "Apply".

With this search, I get 33 results. Due to the small amount of results, I could check them one by one. At the bottom of the search page, it indicates me I have 4 pages worth of results. The number of pages is at the bottom of the screen.

1   2   3   4

Another option would be to add another filter, and see if we still get results or not. In case we don't get any, we remove the last filter we applied.

Let's add another location that interests us to increase the amount of results, since we'll do the Industry filter next and it'll reduce the amount of people by a lot. We also want to add "Barcelona", but it doesn't appear on the list, so we press the + button and we write it, and we select it from the list.

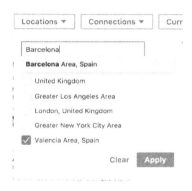

It'll look like this, and we click "Apply".

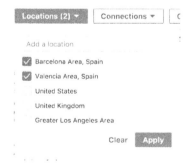

And it throws off 128 people as result.

7.1.5 Searching by industry

Another filter we can add is Industry. To use it, we have to access the screen with all the filter options.

All Filters

And within the screen, we have the "Industries" option.

Industries

Add an industry

Primary/Secondary Education

Health, Wellness and Fitness

Venture Capital & Private Equity

Music

Education Management

I'm going to select "Automotive" and 8 results show up.

If this filtering corresponds to people we're interested in contacting, now we can actually do it, since they're only 8 people. Now what? Once we've contacted them, we deactivate both zones (Valencia and Barcelona), and we activate other zones, so we can contact people with this profile in other parts of the world. Instead of selecting Spain, since the list can become too long.

To contact them, it would be interesting to check each one of the profiles first, without leaving the search. This is the way to do it: we place our pointer on the person's name and we click it with the right button.

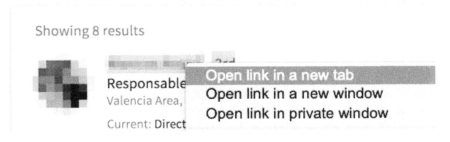

We select, "Open link on a new tab", and then we have our search in one tab with all the people we want to check out / contact, and in another tam, we have the people whose profile we're going to check. When we're done, we close the person's tab and we go back to the general list.

Another way of working could be opening them one by one, the profiles of the 8 people in the results, without closing the search tab. The advantage of doing it this way is that, when we open a different tab for each people, you can check the first profile as the rest of the profiles load.

7.1.6 Excluding results

Let's imagine there are results we wish to exclude, for example, those who correspond to "Export", as we can see in this result.

In this case we're seeing, there's only one, but they could be many more.

We want to make a "Title" exclusion, and there's where we're going to write "-export" without the quote marks. With the - we indicate we don't want that word to appear in the results. Three ways of excluding Export results with different combinations:

Sales -Export

Sales Manager -Export

"Sales Manager" -Export

7.1.7 Multiple search

Another situation we may find ourselves in, is that besides "Sales Manager", we also want "Sales Representative", and we'd have to make two searches, but we can make both searches together, adding "Sales Representative" at the end, including the quote marks, adding the logic operator OR in the middle.

Title

    ʒxport OR "sales representative"

Like this:

"sales manager" –export OR " sales representative"

- "Sales Manager" excluding Export

- And "Sales Representative" Export or not, because we didn't add an exclusion for it.

To also exclude Export from "Sales Representative", the solutions would be adding -export to each of the two options, and it would look like this:

*"Sales Manager" –Export OR "*Sales Representative*" –Export*

If we simplify it, it can be:

("Sales Manager" OR " Sales Representative") –Export

Title

    ' Sales Representative") -Export

And remember to click "Apply", to see the results.

7.1.8 Searching by company

We click the "Clear" option to erase all the filters we applied previously, and starting a new search from scratch.

Next to the search bar at the top, we have the option of filtering by "Companies".

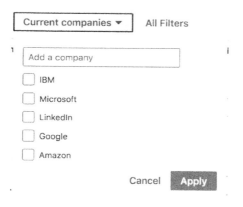

In this case, I'm going to search for the car manufacturer "SEAT".

Current companies ▼   All Filters

SEAT|

SEAT - Sports & Entertainment Alliance in Te...
Sports

Seat King, LLC.
Business Supplies and Equipment

SEAT Planners, Inc.
Events Services

Seat Scouts
Computer Software

SEAT,SA
Automotive

Current companies ▼   All Filters

Add a company

☐ IBM

☐ Microsoft

☐ LinkedIn

☐ Google

☐ Amazon

☑ SEAT,SA

Clear   **Apply**

In my case, it throws these results.

Showing 4,112 results

Now, to reduce the number of results and focus on the ones we're interested in, in the "Title" field, we're going to add "sales". We click "All Filters" and then "Title", we're going to change the search for:

And now these results appear.

Showing 95 results

What I aim for with this whole example is for you to see how to use searches. You have to do them step by step increasingly. Don't make a search in one hit, with all the filter options applied at once, because you won't know which filter left you with no results, like it happened to me before.

7.1.9 Chain search

Another search we can do is by any chain of text we want to look for within the LinkedIn Profile, regardless of the section in which they wrote it.

The way of doing this is writing it directly in the search bar and pressing Enter, or clicking the blue text "See all results".

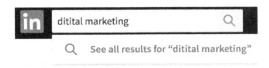

And the results that show up are below. The first thing it shows are job offers, then people who have that text first in their Headline, then in their current position, etc.

7.1.10 Searching through another contact

A very useful feature is accessing other people through our contacts. When we conduct a search or visit a person's profile, LinkedIn shows us which people we have in common, so we can ask for references or to be introduced..

As you can see, this person is our Level 2 and I have 7 people who know them. If we click on the people's photos, a new screen with the list of those 7 people opens, which they have as Level 1 contacts and me too.

Besides, LinkedIn launched a new feature to help us access other people in an easier way. And it's through a new kind of filter.

When we go to the advanced search screen, clicking the magnifying glass, we select "People", then we click "All Filters", and we'll have this option in the screen that appears.

And we type the name of one of our Level 1 contacts, we select it from the list that appears, and we click the "Apply" button on the upper right to see the results.

7.1.11 Three more filters

Other filters we have is Past companies, which works like company search, but to filter people who've worked in a company before.

Past companies

Add a company

☐ IBM

☐ Microsoft

☐ Accenture

☐ Google

☐ Hewlett Packard Enterprise

And by interests.

7.1.12 The search nearly no one knows about

One of the searches that nobody knows about, and the reason is that it's fairly well hidden, is that, besides searching for universities, we have a special search screen within to locate old alumni, which will help us locate that person you're looking for within a company. Since we haven't seen how to search universities yet, which would come first, I'll explain both searches on point "7.3".

7.2 Searching companies

We can also search for companies. On the search bar, we click on "More" and we select "Companies".

We write the text we wish to search in the search box above, and results show.

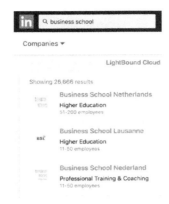

Momentarily, at least, there are no filtering options for company searches in the free versions. Then, when we see the Premium paid version we'll see the options it offers.

Still, this kind of search is very useful, we're going to give you an example. We search for a company and we click on its name, and it'll take us to that company's card.

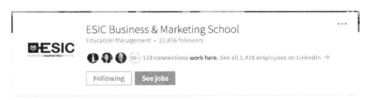

If you're looking for a job, you have the "See jobs" button there, the job positions this company has posted, and above it shows I know 119 people (Level 1) that are employees, and there are 1,419 ESIC employees who've signed up to LinkedIn. We click that blue phrase.

We'll jump to the search screen, with the company option selected and their employees filtered.

Now we have 1,362 results, so we have to filter further to reduce that amount and reach the people who we're actually interested in.

Another way of doing it is the following: we start a new search, clicking "Clear" and we select "People".

We go to the filtering options on the right, and in the filtering option "Current companies", we introduce the name of the company we wish to filter.

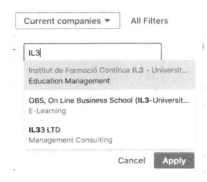

Adding the company, it'll automatically filter all the employees. Depending on the amount they have, we'll have to filter furtherly to reduce the amount.

7.3 University searches

We can also make searches to locate universities and business schools. We click "Schools" on the search bar.

It works like the company searcher and, like with companies, with no filtering options.

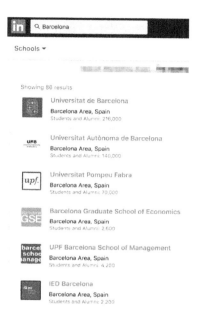

We click the name of a University and we go to its LinkedIn card.

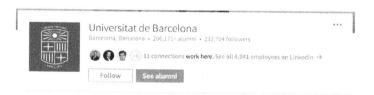

I have 11 people among my Level 1 contacts who work at the Universitat de Barcelona, and the University has 6,941 employees signed up on LinkedIn. We can click any of those figures; the first one will takes us to a search and we'll only see those 11 people, and if we click the other, we'll see what we saw before in companies, but this time with the university.

Since we clicked on 6,941 people who are employees, we going to see exactly the same filtered result we saw in the previous case (company).

So Universities have two kinds of filters applied, by Company, to filter employees, and the other one we're going to see now.

While being in this screen, you'll notice there's a button to see alumni.

And it'll take us to a special search screen to locate alumni from that university. It would be ideal that it's the same University we went to, to have something in common to talk about with the person we locate.

Now let's see how to use this fabulous search tool.

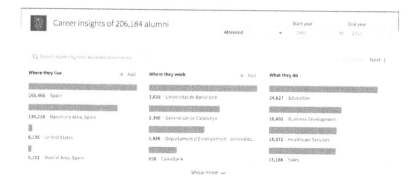

On the top right section we can indicate the range of years in which we want to filter people. Below, we have several types of filters, where we see the volume of contacts there are with colored bars. If we click "Show more", more options drop down.

Let's use it so you can see how useful this search screen is. To select any filter option, we only have to click it.

We click on people who are in the United Kingdom "3.200 United Kingdom"

And then we select people who work at "European Medicines Agency"

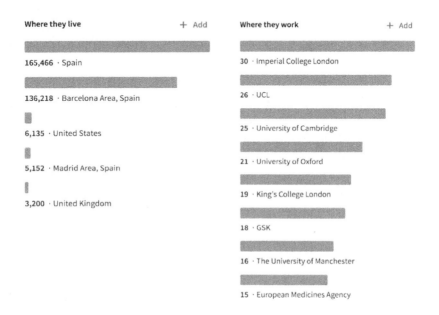

On the top we have the options we're using to filter. If we want to remove any of them, we only have to click the one you wish to remove. The number that appears above is the amount of results we have.

And under the filtering options, we have the list of people who comply with the options we set.

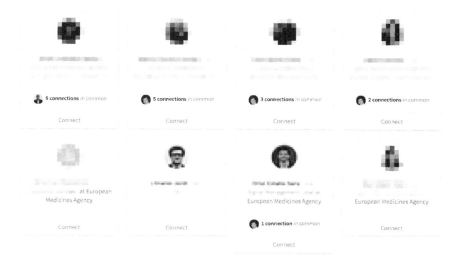

Here we can do the same thing we did before with the right button (opening the people's profiles in different tabs).

Besides the filtering options we saw, there are more. If we click "Next", we'll see the rest of options.

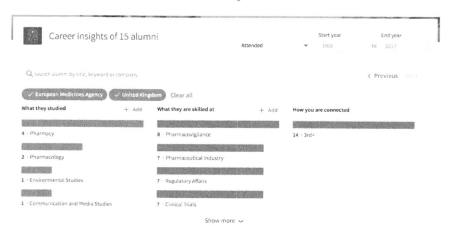

This search screen is one of the great unknowns for a lot of people. When used well, it'll help you open a lot of doors.

7.4 Automatic searches

Currently, the function of saving automatic searches is being remodeled completely. To see how it's used, I'll give you an example in point "**7.5.3 Job offers in your email**", it works the same as people searches, only available in Premium Sales Navigator and Recruiter versions.

7.5 Job searching

Within LinkedIn areas, there's the possibility of posting job offers, and thus we have the opportunity of finding a job.

We click on the search magnifying glass and when we enter the search engine, we click "Jobs".

People   **Jobs**   Content   More ▼

Only by entering, it will show the global total positions currently posted on LinkedIn's platform.

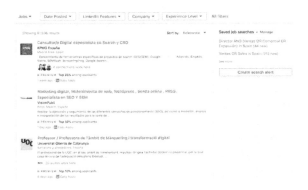

We have the filtering options on the top, in the search bar.

Next, the amount of active job offers appears, based on the filtering options we applied.

We can sort them by Relevance or Date.

7.5.1 Offers' structure

Job offers appear at the left part of the screen.

We see the offered position's title, the company, location, a brief description, and this offer indicates us that, if we apply now, we'll be among the first 10 candidates to apply.

Then it indicates us it was published only 3 days ago, and there's a button called "Easy Apply". This function allows us to upload our on curriculum vitae from LinkedIn and send it to the company, or sending them our LinkedIn Profile. It makes the whole process a lot easier.

Let's see this offer.

We see this offer follows the same scheme, but now there are photos of people. These are people we know who work at that company, so we can contact them for information about the position or which person you must contact.

To see the complete offer you only have to click the blue title where the position name is.

7.5.2 Filters

In the search bar, on the right, we click "All Filters" and this screen will appear.

7.5.2.1 Location

Location allows us to segment the search to the area, region and country where we live, or where we want to move.

Next to each location, you'll notice there is a number; it's the amount of active job offers there are now.

As we've seen before, we can click +Add to write the location we want to search and select it from the list.

Location

Popayan

Popayán, Cauca Department, Col...

☐ Madrid, Madrid, Spain

☐ Badia Del Valles, Catalonia, Spain

☐ Gautegiz Arteaga, Basque Country, Spain

☐ Basetxeta, Basque Country, Spain

7.5.2.2 Company

Another filter we can use is Company; this will help us know all the job offers a concrete company has, and we can add the location filter to know the offers from a company, for example, in our country, in case we're interested in working for that company.

Company

Add a company

☐ Vodafone

☐ Nestlé

☐ TENEA TECNOLOGIAS

☐ KPMG España

☐ Social You, S.L.

7.5.2.3 Date

We can also filter by how long ago the offer was posted. The options here are fixed and we can't modify them.

Date Posted

◯ Past 24 hours

◯ Past Week

◯ Past Month

◉ Any Time

7.5.2.4 Experience

Here we can filter if we're looking for a junior, or more senior position, etc.

Experience Level

☐ Not Applicable

☐ Internship

☐ Entry level

☐ Associate

☐ Mid-Senior level

☐ Director

☐ Executive

7.5.2.5 Industry

If you want to work in an industry concretely, select it from here. If you're open to several sectors, the more filters you add, the less job offers that appear in the results.

Industry

| Add an industry |

☐ Computer Software

☐ Internet

☐ Management Consulting

☐ Marketing and Advertising

☐ Information Technology and Services

7.5.2.6 Offered position

This allows us to filter so there only appear, for example, positions in Marketing, Finances, etc.

7.5.3 Job offers in your email

LinkedIn allows us to automatize searches, and the job search section also works.

7.5.3.1 Creating an alert

Once you've conducted a search with the filters and words you wish to search, on the upper right we have the button to create an alert. This means LinkedIn will email you automatically when any new job offer within the search criteria you enter is posted.

Remember that by clicking "Create search alert" it creates an alert on the current search you've done, and this screen will appear.

The text at the upper left says "Jobs in…" and the filter we applied and below that, it allows us to indicate the frequency in which we want them to send us new offers that are posted and comply with this search.

And at the lower right you can indicate by which means you want to be notified; if you prefer email or as mobile push notification through LinkedIn app, or desktop. I'd leave both options enabled at the beginning, until you know which one is more comfortable for you.

7.5.3.1 Managing alerts

On the screen's upper right we have the alerts manager. Now you'll see I've created three different alerts so you can see them; now you'll see the first one.

Saved job searches • Manage

Director AND (Ventas OR Comercial OR
Expansión) in Spain (8 new)

See more

Create search alert

Now we click "See More" and the rest of them drop down. Next to each one of them, it indicates the amount of new job offers since the last time you checked.

Saved job searches • Manage

Director AND (Ventas OR Comercial OR
Expansión) in Spain (8 new)

Ventas OR Sales in Spain (145 new)

Marketing in Spain (90 new)

(1 new)

(2 new)

(1 new)

(4 new)

(24 new)

(5 new)

(17 new)

See less

Create search alert

We click the "Manage" button, which is at the screen's upper right, and we get to this screen.

Manage search alerts   ✕

Director AND (Ventas OR Comercial OR Expansión) in Spain (8 new)   Edit ⌄   Delete

Ventas OR Sales in Spain (145 new)
Past 24 Hours   Edit ⌄   Delete

Marketing in Spain (90 new)   Edit ⌄   Delete

⬚⬚⬚⬚⬚⬚ (1 new)   Edit ⌄   Delete

⬚⬚⬚⬚⬚⬚ ⬚⬚⬚⬚⬚⬚ (2 new)   Edit ⌄   Delete

⬚⬚⬚⬚⬚⬚ (1 new)   Edit ⌄   Delete

ⓘ You have reached the 10 active search alert limit.   Cancel   [Save]

In the screen that appears, we can manage the alerts we've created, in each one of them it indicates us which search it is for, which location, and the amount of new offers since the last time we clicked it and saw them.

Director AND (Ventas OR Comercial OR Expansión) in Spain (8 new)

At the upper right we have the buttons to delete that alert and editing it.

Edit ⌄   Delete

If we click "Edit", this screen appears.

Director AND (Ventas OR Comercial OR Expansión) in Spain (8 new)   Edit ⌃   Delete

Receive alert   Get notified via

| Daily ▼ | ☑ Email |
| | ☑ Mobile and desktop notification ⓘ |

At "Receive alert", we have a drop-down menu with these options.

Receive alert

✓ Daily
   Weekly
   Monthly

To see the job offers we only have to click the name of the search.

7.5 Content Search

After clicking the magnifying glass, we select the "Content" op.

People   Jobs   **Content**   More ▼

In my case, I've made a search to find posts made in LinkedIn by professionals, about "ESIC IMAT", and all the posts appear. In this case, we see the most relevant.

To put it simply, it's like a content search engine, like Google, within LinkedIn. In this option, we focus on content published by professionals within LinkedIn.

This is another search feature that is very underused by LinkedIn professionals, and the informative potential it can provide us is very high.

Let's see another example, interested in knowing everything that's said about a company? Yours, your competition, a supplier, or a future cliente.

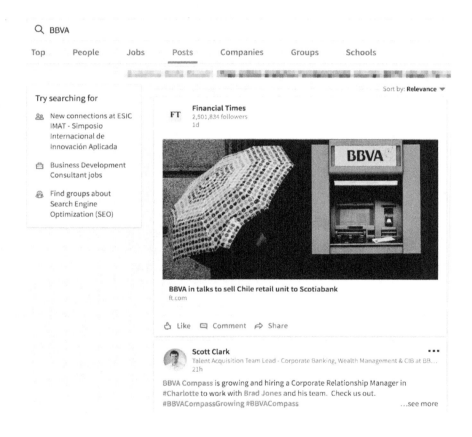

We can also use it to analyze news tendencies that are currently on, about a person concretely, or an event.

Now let's see the posts of a business school, or a university, etc.

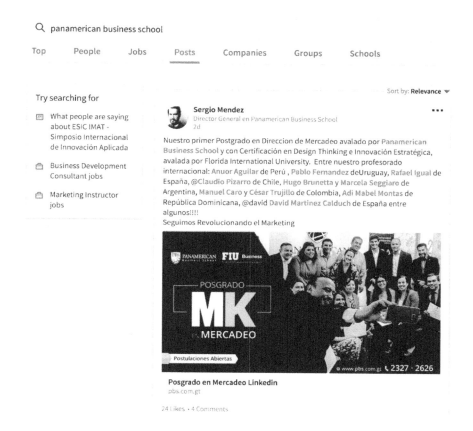

By searching the Panamerican Business School, it throws off posts made by them, and post made by other people talking about them.

7.6 Groups Search

When we click the magnifying glass to make searches, we have the Groups option at the menu bar that appears below.

And it shows us the amount of groups there are, and some groups.

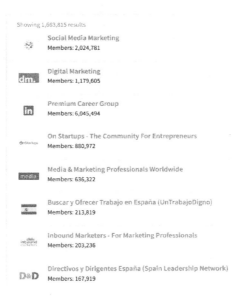

We see there are 1,663,815 groups, and some of them with a lot of people. The first one that shows has over two million members.

There are no filtering options in groups search.

Which groups should we search? Those that could be interesting to us:

- About our company

- About our sector

- From the region/regions where we work

- Related Institutions o Organizations

- Regulations and legislation (is they apply to us)

- Where our clients are

- About our studies, University, Business School, career, Master's

- About the field in which we studied

- Etc.

Chapter 8

Searches with Operators

L inkedIn allows us to perform certain kinds of advanced searches using a series of operators we're going to see.

8.1 Logic operators

Using operators, we'll be able to create much more complex queries, and write them directly in the search box.

("sales director" **OR** salesperson) **AND** IBM **NOT** "consumables"

We're looking for Sales Directors or salespersons, who are from IBM but don't carry consumables.

8.1.1 OR

"sales manager" OR "business developer" OR "key account"

VP OR "V.P." OR "Vice president" OR "Vicepresident"

8.1.2 AND

"sales manager" AND international

8.1.3 NOT

NOT manager

(IBM OR microsoft) NOT google

manager NOT consumables NOT printers

NOT director NOT manager

8.1.4 Parentheses

These will show different results:

(Sales OR Commercial) AND Automotive

Sales OR (Commercial AND Automotive)

The first one throws 68 people and the second one throws 21,095 people.

8.2 Field names

We can also indicate what we want to look for concretely in the title, in the last names, etc.

title:"iOS" **NOT lastname:**diaz **school:**("UNIVERSIDAD POLITECNICA DE VALENCIA" OR UOC)

We must keep in mind that NOT only affects what it has next, therefore, it won't affect schools. If we want to exclude them, we must do this:

title:"iOS" **NOT lastname:**diaz **NOT school:**("UNIVERSIDAD POLITECNICA DE VALENCIA" OR UOC)

You can use: firtsname, lastname, title, company, school.

8.3 More operators

("sales director" **OR** salesperson) **AND** IBM **NOT** "consumables"

("sales director" **OR** salesperson*) **&** IBM - "consumables"

8.4 Execution order

Operators' execution order:

Quote marks ""

Parentheses ()

NOT

AND

OR

8.5 Searches from outside of LinkedIn

In google "site:es.linkedin.com/in/ sales director" so it looks like this:

https://www.google.es/search?client=opera&hs=BK&biw=16 36&bih=859&q=site%3Alinkedin.com%2Fin%2F+sales+director &oq=site%3Alinkedin.com%2Fin%2F+sales+director

With this search from outside of LinkedIn, through Google's search engine, we're telling it to look for 'sales director' (without quote marks), within LinkedIn.

Chapter 9

LinkedIn Sales Navigator

The objective of Sales Navigator is building natural relations with clients to increase our sales. It allows us to locate, in an assisted and almost automatic way, the appropriate people and companies for our objectives. It identifies which ones are truly valuable and lets you interact with them with personalized messages. Without a doubt, if you're in the sales world, you need a Premium Sales account with LinkedIn Sales Navigator.

9.1 LinkedIn Sales Navigator

When we hire the paid Sales Premium Version with Sales Navigator, we'll see we have more features for managing contacts.

My advice is that you apply everything I explained on the previous book and this one first, and when you've been doing it for a while, you can consider the Sales Navigator version. The fact that you spend money doesn't necessarily means you'll sell more.

In case of a sales team, I do recommend the Chief Team or the Top Salesperson has a Premium account, to start learning how to use it, and then acquire more licenses for the rest of the team.

But once again we go back to the paid vs free principle; the limit or increase of effectiveness will depend on the quality of your profile and your contacts agenda.

So you can understand how LinkedIn and Sales Navigator work in an easy way: with LinkedIn's normal version, on the center screen, we see what our contacts post, in my case they're 11,000, plus the professionals, companies and universities I follow.

And in Sales Navigator, we only see the content posted by the professionals and companies we've marked as Leads in the center screen.

The objective is that we focus only on Leads, and don't waste time among all the noise generated by our whole contacts agenda.

On the left we have a filter, on the bottom right we have the profiles we've recently visited and the last searches we've conducted.

And on the top right, we have our Social Selling index, you can consult yours here.

https://www.linkedin.com/sales/ssi

As you can see, the concept is completely different, from the work approach point of view.

In Sales Navigator, there are three versions we can hire

- Sales Navigator Professional

- Sales Navigator Team

- Sales Navigator Enterprise

Here you have a comparison of the three versions

https://davidmcalduch.com/linkedin-sales-navigator-social-selling-la-soluciones-ventas-linkedin/

	FEATURES	LINKEDIN FREE	PREMIUM BUSINESS PLUS	SALES NAVIGATOR PROFESSIONAL	SALES NAVIGATOR TEAM	SALES NAVIGATOR ENTERPRISE
See when prospects check you out	Who's Viewed My Profile	Last 5 people	Last 90 days	Last 90 days	Last 90 days	Last 90 days
Reach prospects directly	InMails (per month)	-	15	20	30	50
	PointDrive presentations (per month)	-	-	-	10	Unlimited
Find the right leads and accounts	Extended LinkedIn Network Access	-	√	√	√	√
	Advanced Sales-Specific Search Tools (see all the filters)	-	-	√	√	√
	Automatic Lead & Account Recommendations	-	-	√	√	√
	Territory Preferences	-	-	√	√	√
Stay organized and up-to-date on leads & accounts you're interested in	Job Change Alerts	-	-	√	√	√
	Prospect & Company News Alerts	-	-	√	√	√
	Notes & Tags	-	-	√	√	√
Training and education	Learning Center	-	-	√	√	√
Leverage LinkedIn wherever you work	Dedicated Mobile App	-	-	√	√	√
	CRM Widgets	-	-	-	√	√
	CRM Sync (with Write-Back)	-	-	-	√	√
Access the entire LinkedIn network	Out-of-Network Unlocks (per month)	-	-	-	25	25
Unlock the power of your company's social graph	Warm Introductions through TeamLink	-	-	-	Team network	Company network
Enterprise Capabilities	Seat Management	-	-	-	Basic	Enterprise-grade
	Usage Reporting	-	-	-	√	√
	Single-Sign-On Integration	-	-	-	-	√
Billing and Support	Volume and Multi-Year Discounts	-	-	-	√	√
	Invoicing	-	-	-	√	√
	Dedicated Relationship Manager	-	-	-	√	√
			Start your free trial	Request free demo	Request free demo	

In this address you have an Evernote notebook where you have this chart and more information so you can check it. If you don't have Evernote (it's free), you can sign up in www.solucionafacil.es/elefante

And to access your Evernote notebook with LinkedIn Sales Navigator, this is the address: https://www.evernote.com/pub/davidmcalduch/linkedinsalesnavigator

Sales Navigator includes these functions:

1. Main Page: the objective of this screen is to keep us up to date with every update from companies and leads, and new relations of those who we've added to Sales Navigator because we're interested in them.

2. Possible Leads and accounts: Sales Navigator allows us to save those people and companies we're interested in with a single click, so we can follow their updates.

3. Recommendations of possible clients: helps us locate new opportunities based on the preferences we've established.

4. Lead Builder: with an advanced system of over 26 filters, it's so much easier and quicker to reach the people we're really interested in.

5. Salesforce Synchronization: allows you to automatically import your accounts and contacts from Salesforce to Sales Navigator.

6. Full access to the whole network: you can see the profiles and activity of your Level 1, 2 and 3 contacts.

7. Unblocked out of network profiles: we can't usually see even the names of out of network profiles but, with Sales Navigator, everything is visible.

8. CRM Widgets: you can check LinkedIn data directly from the screen from your CRM.

9. TeamLink: work in groups to discover hidden contacts.

10. Usage reports: you'll have access to reports of how your team is using Sales Navigator.

11. Includes a Premium Career Subscription: with Sales Navigator Pro, you have access or will have access to the functions to find work opportunities, sending your application, and getting your dream job.

Here you have some guided prices, by person. Remember, yearly payments get you a good discount.

And in this address, you can see the current prices.

https://www.linkedin.com/premium/switcher/sales

When we enter the search section or we conduct a search with Lead Builder, the search screen is completely different.

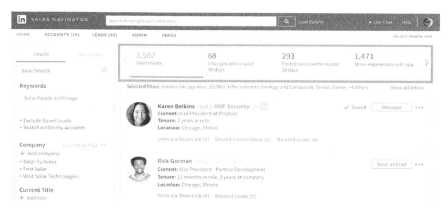

You can see the filters on the left, the search results on the center, and above the results, you can see an information and filtering bar..

Total search results, 68 people have changed their positions in the last 90 days, 293 posts have been done in the last 30 days, etc. When we click them, we see the people of each option.

9.2 Sign-Up Assistant

When we sign up to Sales Navigator, we have access to the new address besides www.linkedin.com. This new address is for sales: www.linkedin.com/sales, and it's the entryway for our Sales Navigator.

The first thing we'll do with Sales Navigator is going through an assistant where we're going to explain which companies, sectors and positions we address, etc.

With all that information, Sales Navigator will help us locate new Leads, and when we select a company, it'll directly tell us which people we have to contact, based on the objectives we've previously indicated.

Every person in your company who hires Sales Navigator must go through this assistant to customize it to their needs and objectives.

Now we're going to see step by step how the assistant is. On the first screen, it welcomes us, and at the bottom right corner we have the button to begin.

On the next screen, it asks us in which geographic zones we're looking for clients. We can indicate everything we need, and they don't have to be in the same country, not even in the same continent. We can add cities, regions and countries.

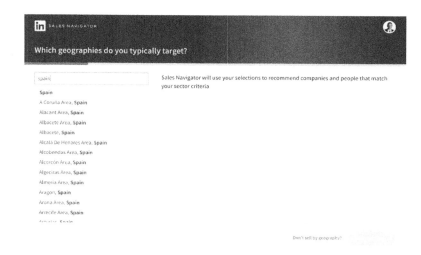

If you don't work geographically, you can indicate so by clicking "Don't sell by geography?" at the bottom right. And once we're done, we click "Continue."

The third screen is where we indicate which sectors we address. Same as the previous window, we can include everything we want. This filter is mandatory; we must include at least one sector. When we're done, we click "Continue".

We get to the screen where we mark which company sizes we address; you can select all that apply, and it's also mandatory to at least select one.

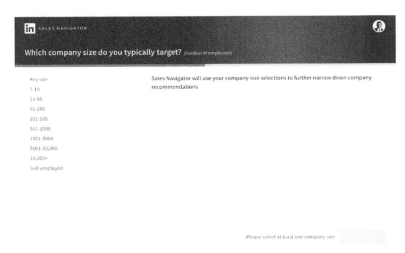

And now we get to the people's functions.

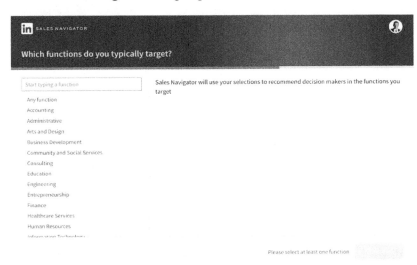

Functions is where we indicate who our contact person is when we contact a company.

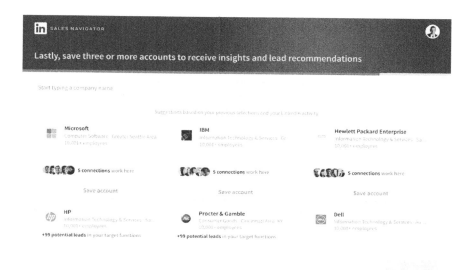

In this last screen, what the Sales Navigator assistant asks is for us to add (you can do searches in this same screen) companies (three minimum), so when we enter the Sales Navigator screen, we can already see news and updates from those companies, to discover new opportunities.

9.3 Work screen in a computer

To access our Sales Navigator, we can do it from two places: entering from www.linkedin.com on the top right menu, the "Sales Nav" option will appear.

And the other way is directly typing the URL www.linkedin.com/sales

In both cases, we'll arrive at the same screen.

On the top, we have the search bar at the center, and below that, we have the menus bar.

At the search bar's right, you can see you have the search magnifying glass and the "Lead Builder" button. They both take us to the same advanced search screen (with over 23 filters).

On the menus bar, we have the "Home" button to go to the main page, "Accounts", which has two options: the accounts we've saved and the ones LinkedIn suggests based on the data we've provided.

We have the "Leads" menu where the people we've saved are.

Then we have the "Inbox" menu, where we can access the Sales Navigator messaging center and the basic LinkedIn inbox.

And last, "Seat Management" from where we can manage all the Sales Navigator licenses we have, in a centralized way.

9.4 Work screen on a Smartphone

We have Sales Navigator available for Android and iOS Smartphones.

Android	iTunes
http://ow.ly/GaD030f24jS	http://ow.ly/XnIR30f24fH

This is Sales Navigator's main screen.

On the top of the screen, we have a search bar. Next to it, we have a wheel for settings, and under that, we have a menu with four options.

If we tap the wheel, it'll take us to the configuration options we've provided when went through the assistant.

On the first option of the "Home" menu, the Leads and accounts posts will appear so we can be up to date with everything they post and when they appear on the news. This works the same as in the computer version.

If we click on one of the people in this screen, it'll show us a special screen with their LinkedIn profile.

You can see that two options that don't exist on LinkedIn free version will appear: tag and add notes.

The second option of the menu shows us possible Lead and accounts Sales Navigator has detected that could be of our interest.

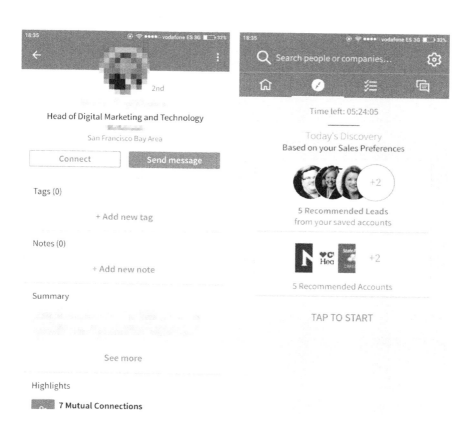

The third option in the menu shows us the activity of our Leads, and offers us several options to see the kinds of actions performed by them.

We also have this information for accounts.

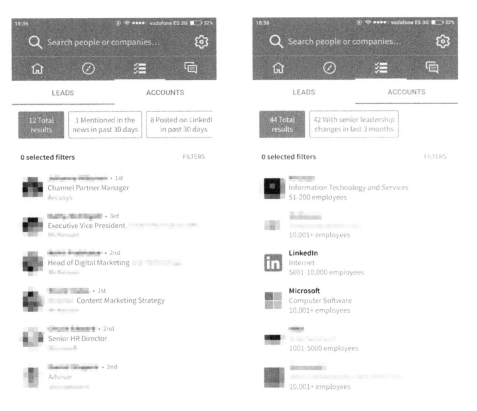

And the fourth option in the menu is Sales Navigator messaging.

9.5 Sales Navigator in Gmail and G-Suite

If you use Google's email system, both the particular Gmail version as well as the corporate G-Suite, we can install a Chrome extension so we can have the Sales Navigator information while we read the emails from our contacts.

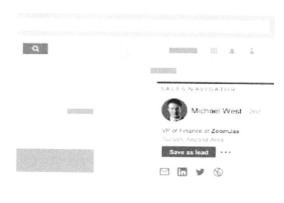

To install this extension you must go to this address from Chrome in your computer: http://ow.ly/YRS430f216N

9.6 Sales Navigator in Microsoft Dynamics CRM

Up to the purchase of LinkedIn by Microsoft, LinkedIn only had integration with Salesforce on a CRMs level. But now it has also been integrated to Microsoft Dynamics CRM, besides being able to install an extension to keep LinkedIn data and searches within Dynamics.

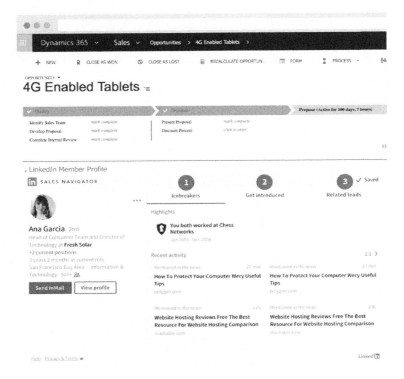

Here's the address to download it.

http://ow.ly/xQFB30f21AA

9.7 PointDrive

One of the problems when sending information to a client via email is that we need to know:

- When they've opened the email.

- When they've opened the attachments and how much time they've dedicated to read them.

- In case the person forwards the email to other people in their organization and access the documents, knowing who they are.

To solve this problem; LinkedIn acquired the company PointDrive to integrate it to their Sales Navigator solution on July 26 2016.

With PointDrive, we create an access portal for our clients and contacts. This portal is responsive. The screen is customizable with your contents, including videos.

When our contacts access (by emails, with documents, etc...) Sales Navigator grants us statistics with this portal.

We can see the amount of visits each document has, the total time they spent seeing it and the amount of downloads.

By entering one of the documents to see the information with more detail, we can see the people that have interacted with the document; and on the right we can go to Sales Navigator to see their profile or their recent activity.

PointDrive is available for LinkedIn Sales Navigator Team and Enterprise accounts.

Chapter 10

Final Tips

I hope you've followed my advice and applied everything we've seen in this book. If you have, now you can use this book as a reference book.

If you liked this book, I encourage you to give your opinion at Amazon

https://davidmcalduch.com/libro02linkedin

And, if you want to continue advancing in your knowledge, you can continue with the rest of the books in this series: www.lasclavesde.com/linkedin

Made in the USA
Monee, IL
27 June 2023

37815572R00142